WE ARE ANTIFA

EXPRESSIONS AGAINST FASCISM, RACISM AND POLICE VIOLENCE IN THE UNITED STATES AND BEYOND

The work within is the intellectual property of the contributors and the views expressed therein are those of the contributors. Copyright © 2020 Into the Void and individual contributors.

All rights reserved. No part of this publication may be reproduced, stored in a retrieval system, or transmitted, in any form or by any means, electronic, mechanical, photocopying, recording or otherwise, without the prior permission of the contributor.

Library and Archives Canada Cataloguing in Publication

Title: We are Antifa : expressions against fascism, racism and police violence in the United States
 and beyond / edited by Heath Brougher, Philip Elliott, Amanda Gaines, Jay C. Mims, Andrew Rihn.
Names: Brougher, Heath, 1979- editor. | Elliott, Philip, 1993- editor. | Gaines, Amanda, 1994-
 editor. | Mims, Jay C., 1991- editor. | Rihn, Andrew, editor.
Description: Poetry and prose.
Identifiers: Canadiana (print) 20200269461 | Canadiana (ebook) 20200319485 | ISBN 9781999086817
 (softcover) | ISBN 9781999086824 (Kindle)
Subjects: LCSH: Fascism—Literary collections. | LCSH: Anti-racism—Literary collections. | LCSH:
 Racism—Literary collections. | LCSH: English literature—21st century. | LCSH: Police brutality—
 Literary collections.
Classification: LCC PR1151 .W4 2020 | DDC 810.8/03581—dc23

Typeset: Crimson Text
Published in Vancouver, B.C., Canada, by Into the Void
Designed by Into the Void
www.intothevoidmagazine.com

This book is dedicated to all those who have fought for, and are fighting for, justice, equality, and freedom of expression.

CONTENTS

FOREWORD / xi
ABOUT THIS BOOK / xiii
CREATIVE NONFICTION / 3

How the Living Watch the Dead by Cree N. Pettaway / 5
We Were Young, But Not Afraid by Joshua Fernandez / 19
Brother, by Rebecca Frost / 25
Dry Lightning by M. J. Ridley / 33
A Part of the Conversation by Michael J Moore / 43

FICTION / 47

Guide to Straightening by Emily Capers / 49
Into the Weeds by Tim Jones / 57
Children of Children by Blake L. Bell / 63
From the Mountain by Priyanthini Guns / 69
A Policeman of You by Daniel Nathan Horn / 77
Not Racist or Anything, but... by Bill Wilkinson / 83

A Reasonable Fascist by Matt Harris / 105

Headless and Hands by Josh Wagner / 113

The Philanthropist by Sam Palmer / 121

The Bridge by Lin Lucas / 125

West of Nogales, AZ by Charles Duffie / 135

Good Cop by Jeff Ewing / 147

POETRY / 151

the one where the roughnecks burn the world to the ground while looking fab as fuck by Kanyinsola Olorunnisola / 153

Coffin at Dusk by Jonathan Endurance / 157

Fill in the Blanks by James Redfern / 161

Discriminating by Larry Smith / 165

Villain Villanelle by Edward Moreta Jr. / 169

The Peace Sculpture Wore: October, 1996 by Andrés Castro / 173

At Nightfall by Thea Matthews / 179

A President like No Other by Alan Meyrowitz / 183

Lead and Testicles by Ramon Jimenez / 187

I Can't Breathe: Attica Peace Treaty by Jonathan Andrew Pérez, Esq. / 191

Brutality by Geoffrey Aitken / 197

Abracadabra by Renoir Gaither / 201

This Rage Is a Necessary Monster by Connor Drexler / 205

Magnolia State by Gary Bloom / 209

Itemizing My Identity by Rhea Dhanbhoora / 213

Civil Insubordination, or Where in Amerikkka Are Black People Safe from Racism? by henry 7. reneau, jr. / 217

Thousands of White Allies by John Streamas / 221

Messengers by Richard Hoffman / 225

White Privilege by AE Hines / 229

#StephonClark by Nancy Christopherson / 235

Not All Wolves by Lisa Olsen / 239

Bruna Boscana, Pararge Aegeria *(Linnaeus, 1758)* by Laurence O'Dwyer / 243

An Open Letter to the School Resource Officer Who Almost Shot Me in My Class by Matthew E. Henry / 247

Autoimmune by Vasiliki Albedo / 251

On Sectarianism by Mariana Mcdonald / 255

Ghetto Youth by Darriel McBride / 259

Knee on the Neck by Pèlúmi Sàlàkọ́ / 267

CONTRIBUTOR BIOS / 271

FOREWORD

THESE ARE DARK TIMES, BUT THEY ARE HOPEFUL times. Here at *Into the Void* we've been watching hundreds of thousands of Americans standing up for the rights of people of color and fighting for a better life for all. We wanted to add our contribution to the struggle for justice and equality, so we decided to publish an anthology collection of poetry and prose with 100% of the proceeds donated to Black Lives Matter Toronto. This book is the result.

I want to thank every writer with work inside these pages. Without you, this book could not exist, and without your astounding writing this book would not be the fantastic collection it has become. While your words printed herein may not prevent the murder by police of George Floyd and countless others like him or evict fascists from the White House, your words are far from futile. Fascism, like cancer, grows strong in silent darkness while we look the other way. Fascism seeks to crush dissent by silencing it. Because words, persistent and loud, topple regimes.

Anti-fascism, or Antifa, began where fascism began: Italy. In 1921, the formation of a group named *Arditi del Popolo*

(The People's Daring Ones) saw unionists, anarchists, socialists, communists, republicans and ex-army officers join forces to fight the violent blackshirts supporting Benito Mussolini, who the following year became the fascist dictator of Italy.[1] Years later, while attempting to flee Italy, Mussolini was captured and, on April 28, 1945, executed for his crimes against his country and countrymen. Adolf Hitler learned of his fascist ally's death while cowering in his Führerbunker beneath the city of Berlin as the Soviets, ravenous for revenge, closed in. Two days after Mussolini's execution, Hitler committed suicide as Berlin burned above him.

Anti-fascists in 1921 knew then as contemporary anti-fascists know now that fascists cannot win until all opposition is silenced. Our words remain our first and most powerful weapon against those who would place us in chains and plunge our nations into hate and blood, fear and division, war and genocide. Words are invincible—as long as we never stop using them.

Thank you, contributors of *We Are Antifa*, for using them.

Thank you, my fellow editors, for carefully selecting and shaping them.

Thank you, readers, for valuing and amplifying them.

Philip Elliott
Editor-in-Chief
Into the Void
09/10/2020

---

[1] Paraphrased from "A Brief History of Anti-Fascism" by James Stout in *Smithsonian*, June 24, 2020.

ABOUT THIS BOOK

THE TITLE *WE ARE ANTIFA* IS A RESPONSE TO DONALD Trump's declaration that the United States will be designating Antifa a terrorist organization. This makes no sense because Antifa is not an organization; at its most basic it's a term given to anyone who opposes fascism. Therefore, we are Antifa and we are terrorists.

This is perhaps the most dangerous comment Trump has yet made, his public declaration that he is a fascist. Already, it's had huge effect. On-the-ground protesters and activists are now saying that F.B.I. is interviewing arrestees regarding their connection to "anti-fascist sentiment." On June 3, an opinion piece by Republican senator Tom Cotton was published in *The New York Times* calling for the deployment of the military in order to dominate dissenters. Two days before this, Cotton declared on Twitter that protesters should be killed: "No quarter for Insurrectionists."

This is where we are now: a fascist calls for the murder of protesters and gets an op-ed in the *Times* while out-of-control police roams the streets terrorizing and brutalizing peaceful protesters. Trump himself had peaceful protesters tear-gassed and beaten outside the White House on live TV in a brutal warning to Americans that he has the police and military behind him, that he will use lethal force, and that dissent will be crushed. The danger of all this can't be overstated: not only has fascism arrived in the United States—it's winning.

We encourage our readers to read the excellent "A Brief History of Anti-Fascism" by James Stout in *Smithsonian*, June 24, 2020, to better understand why we are publishing this anthology and how anti-fascism and anti-racism are inextricably linked in the fight against oppression and supremacy.

WE ARE ANTIFA

edited by

Heath Brougher
Philip Elliott
Amanda Gaines
Jay C. Mims
Andrew Rihn

CREATIVE NONFICTION

HOW THE LIVING WATCH THE DEAD

by

Cree N. Pettaway

NEARLY FOUR MONTHS BEFORE THE JUSTICE FOR Victims of Lynching Act passes to declare lynching "the ultimate expression of racism in the United States," Mama, Aunt Willfred, and I stood inside The Legacy Museum in Montgomery, Alabama. The museum is less than six months old, but it carries so much of its history weighed down on the bones of a slave warehouse. I am not necessarily expecting to feel peace in this warehouse while watching hologram reenactments of hunted and incarcerated Blacks, especially considering that the warehouse is between a slave market and a train station that trafficked thousands of slaves through the area. I am also not expecting to be burdened by the presence of any of the people touring the museum alongside me. In my experience, people treat museums like libraries, quiet spaces to tiptoe around and comb through data. Unlike a library, none of the knowledge I check out at The Legacy Museum will be free.

Thirty minutes in, my family and I are watching a montage of statistics and photographs on a miniature screen while a white man stands behind us clutching his rosary and weeping. I'm confused as to what exactly he's crying over, eyeing him, then Mama and Aunt Willfred to see if I'm the one missing something. Mama and Aunt Willfred's eyes confirm my confusion. The three of us are missing something, because we stare at the same images and read the same words he does but shed not one tear. In the two hundred times in history Congress considers anti-lynching laws before actually passing one, and the possible two hundred times in my life I am confronted with discussions of lynching, I don't think I cry once. Who told this man, seeing this torturous history laid out in front of him, that he had permission to cry over what I had not?

In his musings about The Legacy Museum, author Maurice Ruffin notes that the "perpetrators of these terrors are rarely seen, which is appropriate." Weeping rosary man is, to me, a perpetrator. He's not a perpetrator of terror, but of what I deem to be a lack of basic consideration for how much attention he's pulling from a space meant to concentrate on remembering Black people. His parents didn't teach him the importance of when to be seen and not heard. I'm a Black woman, but I do not own Black people, nor the memories others hold of us. I will make that much clear. And therefore, by extension, I do not own and dictate how white people react to the Black people in this museum, whether in photos, holograms, voice, or even in person. I don't like that this man doesn't know that this is not the place for his loud mourning.

In a town nearby, five months before I mentally dare this man to stop grieving these colored lives so loudly, four of seven children reflected on their father's 1947 lynching. This lynching happens 169 miles from my hometown. It is one of sixty recorded lynchings where a victim is "hanged, shot, beaten and burned to death" in or near Montgomery between 1877 and 1950. One of about three hundred lynchings for Alabama within a century after slavery is abolished. At The National Memorial for Peace and Justice, a counterpart to The Legacy Museum, I possibly see this man's name, Elmore Bolling, etched into a steel pillar with other names who have undergone similar terrors. I use the word "possibly" because I assume Bolling's name is there—it should be there—but don't come across it in the photos I take for Grandma Rosa, whose arthritis hinders her from making the trip.

I see Bolling's name at The Legacy Museum, stamped on a jar of soil that reads, "Elmore Bolling, Lowndesboro, AL, December 4, 1947." The soil in Bolling's jar is evidence that he lived, blossomed, and died on the same dirt road. Bolling's family says they believe his hanging was a result of his "prosperity." This prosperity came from hauling kindling and metal, trucking cattle, transporting farmer's milk to dairy processors, and owning a general store his wife Bertha Mae managed while he transported goods during the day. According to family members, Bolling's killer was a man he trusted and did business with, who came into his store to speak with him hours before the murder. Bolling's presumed killer claimed Bolling insulted his wife. Whether true or not, an insult is not worth a man's life. Not worth his wife and children anticipating his evening arrival only to learn that he has been shot and hung yards away from his business and home. Not worth the soil below his dangling feet being jarred and shelved for white people to pay money to stare at.

Less than a mile from Bolling's jar at The Legacy Museum are plaques lingering along the walls of the National Memorial for Peace and Justice that tell the story Bolling's name doesn't. "A Black man was lynched in Millersburg, Ohio, in 1892 for 'standing around' in a white neighborhood," one plaque states. Another: "General Lee was lynched in Reevesville, South Carolina, in 1904 for knocking on a white woman's front door." For me, these claims fall in the same category Bolling's supposed insult does. It is not necessary to say how mundane and obtuse these accusations are when reflecting on them in the 21st century, even in a nation that builds memorials for the dead faster than creating laws to prevent more of them. Am I, like the man strangling his rosary in his fist, meant to cry over the ways these men have died, the ways a people have died, or cry over the sadistic hilarity of the crimes pinned against these named Black people? Or am I to cry of joy over knowing that perhaps some white man, or even my colored self, will learn something about why these Black people should have been able to live? But I cry here neither. Perhaps what irritates me the most about Rosary Man's crying is that I have no comprehension of how to associate it with his knowledge about the slaying of Negros. What does he know about what we both see and learn that I don't?

Why, exactly, is he crying?

Sometime before, on a visit to The History Museum of

Mobile, less than three miles from my house, my mother and I roam about an exhibit most memorable for its recreation of the shackled feet of slaves on the bottom of a ship. As we work our way through the exhibit an elderly white man tells us, "This is sad." This much of course is obvious. My mother and I nod and stare at him, waiting perhaps for the story behind what we've all gathered. He goes on to admit that he's from Ohio and is essentially unfamiliar with the details of violence against Black people. He seems too old to be so ignorant. But there are things I should know that I don't.

Maybe Rosary Man is from Ohio. Maybe he grew up with a Black person here and a Black person there. He knows that elements of their history are sad, it being his history too, but never had the whole horrific narrative thrown at him until his visit to The Legacy Museum. Possibly this man, before coming to the museum, was like many of my students who know of lynchings but can put no names or faces to the act.

In class one day I ask my students, "Do you know who Emmett Till is?" after having them read an essay that discusses the ways whites can distort Black pain. Less than half of my seventeen students know anything about Till, a fact appalling to me given that a significant portion of them are from Louisiana, where I teach and they hopefully learn, one of four states with the most lynchings in the nation. Till, fourteen at the time of his slaying in 1955, had his eyes gouged out, was shot in the back of the head, tied by the neck to a cotton gin with barbed wire, and thrown in a river, all for allegedly flirting with and groping a white woman. This white woman, Carolyn Donham, would reveal in an interview in 2008 that while she cannot recall exactly what happened during her encounter with Till, he never "grabbed her around the waist and uttered obscenities" and "nothing that boy did could ever justify what happened to him." Donham's confession would not become public knowledge until the release of Duke University professor Timothy B. Tyson's book, *The Blood of Emmett Till*, in 2017.

I explain my frustration with my students to my Grandma Rosa who says, "Well, they weren't alive when all that happened."

"Neither was I."

"Yeah, but you read a lot." As a graduate student and a teacher of English and creative writing students, I am required to read, or at least thoroughly skim, as often as I breathe and shit. So, Grandma Rosa is right that I am spoiled when it comes to knowledge of terrors. However, I don't think my students' problems are not reading enough, but rather not being taught how to occasionally read beyond their comfort zones. I try to be this teacher for my students, the teacher that makes them look outside of themselves as much as they look within. But I don't want to be the only one asking them to do this.

Emmett Till's murder happened 294 miles from my home, but I know his story as thoroughly as Michael Donald's. Donald was a nineteen-year-old Black man whose 1981 hanging took place at the corner of a street posthumously named after him. This street served as a partial backdrop for my middle and high school years. My most profound memory of hearing about Donald is riding down his avenue in high school on a bus headed back from a cow auction with my Southern Culture class. Had Donald and Till been alive a couple of hundred years prior they may have been auctioned off in the same way I saw heifers pranced around a caged-in ring and bid on by men in cowboy hats with tucked-in button-down shirts and gritty steel-toe boots. Unlike the heifers, Till and Donald were saved from a stranger's hand publicly inserted into their rectum while high schoolers twisted their heads from side-to-side in cringing confusion as they vowed not to eat a hamburger for the rest of the week. But then again—what is more morbid? A violated cow sold at auction for milk or steak, perhaps just some cow-tipping shenanigans, or a young Black man and Black boy beaten and thrown in a river or strung up on a tree, the newspaper pictures of their mauled bodies the most prominent evidence of their existence?

I do not get too far into the gruesome details of Till or Donald's murders with my students, but I do try to use the micro amount of space in the grey, windowless prison of a classroom I teach in to help them learn about people like Till and Donald so that they, at the very least, are never in a museum crying because they are ignorant. To allow them to put names and faces to Black necks that have slit and snapped and been cried about too late or not at all. Because who but colored me, but my people, will continue to do this lifting for them?

When I google images of a morbidly beaten Till for my students I feel slightly ashamed for allowing them, even as college students, to see the graphic images without permission slips signed by guardians. I cannot recall my reaction when I first saw the swollen misshapenness of Till's face. Had anyone warned me of what I would see the way I do for my students? Told me that I could close my eyes or look away or leave the room if I needed to? There isn't much commentary from my students about the images of Till. I don't think anyone says a word. Then I pull up artist Dana Schutz's "Open Casket" portrait of Till.

It is worth noting that Schutz is a white woman, a particularly significant fact given Schutz's depiction of Till in his casket has been characterized as "an injustice to the Black community" because the "subject matter is not Schutz's." Over two years after the release of this painting I'm still uncertain as to which side of the line I agree with. My students, however, have no confusion on the matter.

"Technically she can paint whatever she wants because of First Amendment rights," one student shouts out. "But I wouldn't do it."

That becomes the statement of the day: "I wouldn't do it." I don't know if it's my presence as a Black woman or them wanting to assure themselves that they, a predominately white group, are racially conscious and sensitive and have no plans of co-opting Black pain as their own. Admittedly, I have set them up and primed them for such a response. Their homework due for the day was to answer the question "Who owns Black pain?" Most respond: "Black people." The question itself is maybe unfair; Who can "own" something as distinct yet untouchable as a person's pain?

In her defense on the subject of her empathy, Schutz says, "I don't know what it is like to be Black in America, but I do know what it is like to be a mother. Emmett was Mamie Till's only son. The thought of anything happening to your child is beyond comprehension. Their pain is your pain." I can relate to

Schutz on an extremely micro level being that I am an aunt of three and a sister of two. When my nieces started potty training, I was excited as their parents were for them to get a reward for not soiling their diapers. When my sister is bullied at school, I am first in line to whoop anybody's butt because, as I tell her, "I'm not afraid to fight children." And when my sister-in-law calls my brother out of his name, I'm willing, although surely incapable, to brawl in the streets with her too.

On that most basic level, I understand Schutz's ability to in some ways relate to the pain of other mothers. But why then not paint a portrait of Mamie Till, fingers intertwined with a slender man pressing his fingers into the dough of her upper arm, while he stares at the camera in fear and something else—insecurity maybe? Why not paint Mamie Till in her sleeveless dress, adorned in giraffes and various unidentifiable abstract lines, a stillness in her eyes that is betrayed and contradicted as soon as she looks down on her son's casket at his funeral? I initially think the dress a bold and busy choice for a grieving mother to wear, as if she is preoccupied with such concerns. But perhaps she is and considers this dress to speak the same conflicting emotions that I feel when I look at her—that she is a woman who must be overwhelmed by grief, yet she is sound enough to know how to draw attention to herself in a way that will get her point across—that as Till's mother she is a part of the performance of what has happened to him. This is the image I want to see Schutz or someone more capable pull apart: how the living watch the dead, and how the living play the part of spectators and spectated. How mothers observe their deceased children. How white people watch slain bodies of Black people they never met. Bodies that, if things had worked out for the Confederacy, they would "own."

"I can't even tell that that's his face," one student says. I am most interested in my students' willingness to comment on Till in the painting rather than Till in photographs that first appear in *Jet*. Has someone before me come along and told them that they could provide commentary on the abstractness of Black pain but not the real thing because they didn't "own" it? Or did Schutz's painting provide them with the necessary distance to feel like they could offer some observations on the publicity and affairs of Blacks? My money is on the latter. Essentially, they are probably staying within their comfort zones of dissecting abstracts as opposed to dissecting the torment of actual faces. But is this not what I'm asking the spectator with his rosary to do? To less vocally lament over the savageness of Black death? I am. But I'm asking him to not mourn now because it's something I wanted him to do before I was watching, before we were in this public space and I had to confront that while his crying is a disturbance, it's the subject matter of his world too, and he has no obligation to wait on my tears to catch up.

What I really want is for white people to be more conscious of how they take up space. Yes, this crying man "technically" has the right to make a fool out of himself if he pleases, whether it be mourning over what his white ancestors have done or failed to do, what his white self has done or failed to do, or because the history he learns strikes him so deep. Regardless of whose fault it is that slavery happened, that lynching happened, that the abuse to Black people is still happening, all of these historical moments have intertwined the Black and white races in inseparable ways. This fact alone gives this man permission to cry in this space. But this doesn't keep me from wanting him to check to see if I have been able to grieve first. At The National Memorial for Peace and Justice visitors exit past a quote from Toni Morrison emphasizing the importance of Black men's and women's throats. As I recall it now, the words make me all too aware of how neglectful I have been in praising my own: "Hear me, they do not love your neck unnoosed and straight. So love your neck; Put a hand on it, grace it, stroke it and hold it up. And all your inside parts that they'd just as soon slop for hogs you got to love them." With this bit of reflection at the end of the memorial's self-guided tour, I still do not cry for Donald, even now when thinking of him as potential food scraps for farm animals.

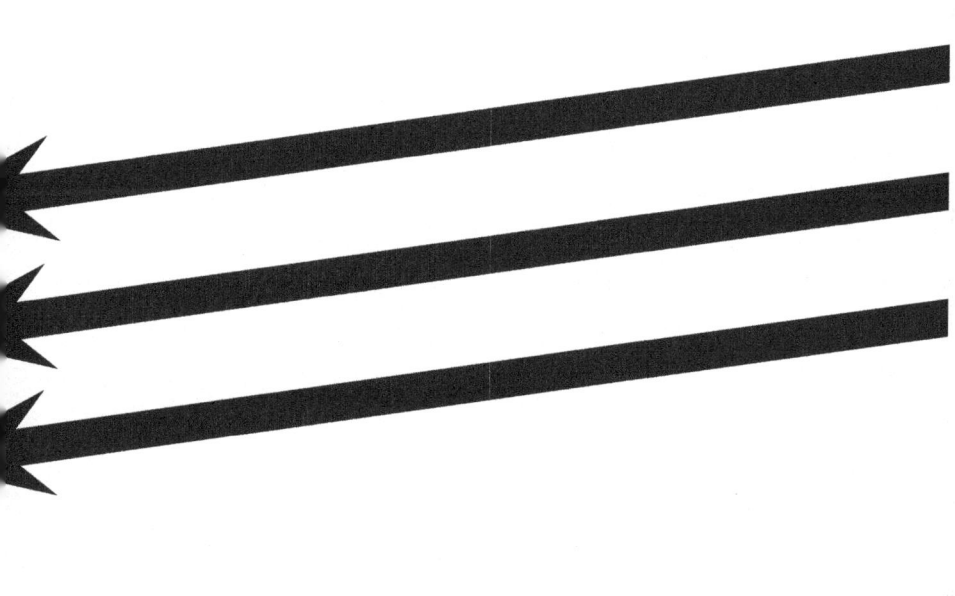

WE WERE YOUNG, BUT NOT AFRAID

by

Joshua Fernandez

WE MARCHED ALONG K STREET IN AN UNRULY LINE, chanting out-of-sync rhymes in cracking voices—rejects with fucked-up haircuts, a trail of cops following close behind, hands clutching their batons like G.I. Joes.

"An! Anti! Antifascista! An! Anti! Antifascista!" we screamed, until out of nowhere three bald heads appeared and we stopped, mouths agape, as if nobody realized what we were protesting against: actual people in uniform, boots and braces and swastikas tatted in blue ink.

They screamed, "White power!" holding their middle fingers up to the crowd.

We watched them watching us and the space in between us grew into its own city of volatile ideas.

We had no weapons—no bats or knives or sticks—only our voices, held like black flags under the California sun. I found a Coca-Cola in my backpack, the red can—12 ounces of high glucose, its elegantly sloped cursive, iconic as an American flag—and I hurled it at the closest bonehead I saw. I remember my uncle telling me that Coca-Cola was once medicine, that it helped calm the souls of the terminally nervous, a wonder tonic, an odd mix of cocaine and caffeine, and I laughed at the image of nervous old people jittering around the world, coked out of their goddamn minds, thinking that they knew it all while they killed themselves slowly, one bottle at a time.

The can sailed through the air like a little red fighter plane, crash landing onto the Nazi's cheek bone and opened a gash the size of a fist, blood spilling, soaking his white t-shirt. The police stood still in confusion, the bonehead wiping the blood, his red hands glowing under the sun and he smiled and took a solid step toward us, but his knees gave out and he fell hard to the concrete. One of his friends rushed to help, the other, a weirder one, launched a Sieg Heil high above his head and I half-wondered if that was a common reaction when his reflexes were tested, like at his general practitioner's office after the rubber mallet banged under his knee.

The other bonehead ran off like a normal person and disappeared behind the Bank of America. We cheered and laughed as the hurt Nazi tried to get up, and please don't tell anyone, but I felt a little sorry for the guy as he laid there, crumpled on the lightrail tracks, greasy yellow and red like a discarded bag of McDonald's.

A woman from the street dropped her Macy's bag and wagged a finger in my direction. "Who are the real Nazis?" she said, pointing at one of our banners that read, ANTI-RACIST

ACTION. Then she turned toward the police and demanded an arrest, but they were frozen by idiocy, still sweating under their thick blue uniforms, all of them probably younger than I am today.

Then, I was sixteen, and I'd only fucked once and still had some baby fat. In my room I hung a crossed-out swastika and my mom made me take it down.

"We don't have to worry about Nazis," she said. "There are no Nazis anymore."

She was a good mom who kept Snickers bars and sodas in the refrigerator. Nobody cared about health back then. In my world of boots and braces and shows at vets halls on the weekends, Nazis were everywhere, like hideous, hard-backed cockroaches, only coming out at night. My mom made a life for us outside all that, tucked away in the suburbs, as far away from East L.A. as she could get.

When the sirens blared that day, we dropped our banners and took a hard left through the alley, the cops giving chase for a while, but fizzling out. They couldn't keep up or got bored and nobody went to jail and we all met up later at a hardcore show in the basement of a rented house, fifty teenagers circling the room like blood cells racing toward a fresh cut. The first band's singer wore a dog collar and screamed about chaos and destruction as the room steamed and filled with the stench of angry adolescents who stomped around endlessly kicking and punching each other for fun. The show stopped short when a cruiser pulled up. Its familiar lights and the barking of orders from a megaphone gave us a thrill, I think. We lived for the opposition. Once again, we scrambled—out the back door, over the fence and into the night we went running and laughing and cursing, like soldiers' ritual after a great, bloody war.

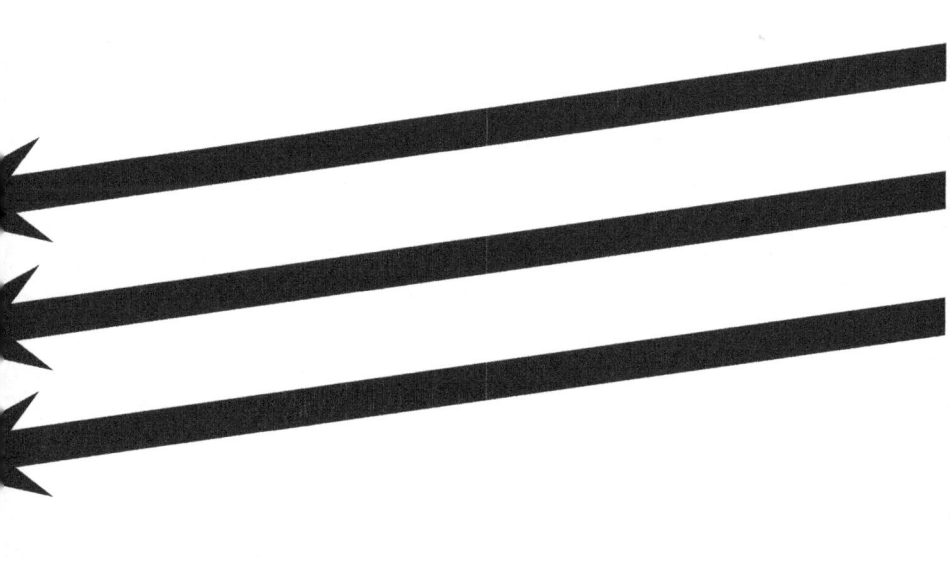

BROTHER,

by

Rebecca Frost

SOMETIMES I COME HOME JUST TO CRY. IT'S THE tenderness of it, the leak stains on my bedroom ceiling, the little pictures of birds, the sage to ward off bad spirits. It's a cliché thing, I think. Like crying at a movie. I smell Mom's hair on the living room pillows, I strum the guitars to see how Dad's tuned them, I listen for your feet upstairs, and I cry messily and quietly touching everything. The dust on it all making me feel heavy and small.

I go into your room. Just to see. When I flip the switch, will the black light come on? When I open your closet, will I see a new skirt stashed in the corner? Have you gotten on laxatives again? I look at Little Deadpool on your bookshelf or the mask you sculpted when you were fifteen, a wicked, sorrowful demon's face.

When you caught me last time, whimperingly drunk, you

crouched beside me on the floor and whispered, "What?"

I didn't know how to share with you the stages of my grief. How, abandoned by more than some hypothetical picture of America, but by my countrymen, I wanted someone to look me in the eyes and explain every upturned word used to invoke the image of our grandmother's fervent, brown face as she sat (fourteen in a subway car) working on the sound of her English.

Who were *the* people, if such a people had ever been, if not irrevocably each other's? Irrevocably America's?

And who were we if not irrevocably people?

It all seemed like a joke in an English film I just didn't fucking get.

It broke my heart in a way I could not explain save to cry and reach for my loveliest thing.

You.

Looking like a little fox, your curls pulled into an anxious ponytail, ready to burst, like us under that childhood roof. I knew the look. I was wearing it, too.

Dad said you looked like a woman. Mom said I was sounding militant.

They were both, always, terrified of what we'd face in the real, live world.

That I'd be shot at a rally waxing philosophical.

That you'd disappear into the marsh after changing into hot pink short shorts in the Walmart bathroom.

Tuesday night, 2016, I watched Florida on my television with those fervent eyes, those despondent eyes, of a disillusioned child. I watched that purple place where we played until the asphalt burned calluses into our feet, where we hunted for

BROTHER,

snakes and alligators, where the limits on our freedom were only so staunch as our own minds and the last good branch that could hold our weight. I watched, prayer twisting my mouth closed, knowing that when Florida rose it would rise like a furious swell from the Atlantic.

That it would engulf you and protect you and you would be safe.

And when it did not rise, when the sweltering sea scape of enigmatic mangroves, our anklebiter anthologies, went red, my roommate and I held each other in a visceral cradle.

I whispered your name as she whispered her bothers' names. As if that alone, benedictions in a church built of devastated limbs, could shelter you.

Our brothers. Disabled and gay and brown and transitioning.

We were afraid and we were vicious, imagining you sacrificed at the altar of this Land.

Our Land.

Your Land.

When you caught me last time, your mouth made this startled little O. Neither of us should have been up so late. Mom made collection calls before I came back for donations of strictly kept promises. No politics. Bedtime at a reasonable hour. Nothing but calm voices around you.

You were different now.

Sometimes you'd scream. Others you'd sit quietly. Staring. Waiting for hours on something you couldn't describe.

A feeling, maybe. An idea. A way for things to make sense, to feel safe, again.

She said, "He's not being an ass, just a little 'perger's.'"

I think you'd wholly believed America was making good on its promise: justice. But you could smell the acrid smell of slaughter and fear rotting in our country's mouth.

The breadth of humanity's shame dawned slowly on you, and maybe the sharp light of it, the unfettered truth of it, made you wish to unknow, to unsee, to unlearn, while ignorance, sweet and fleeting as the memory of a dream, slipped away from you anyway.

I learned about it from Dad, who has spent years quizzing me on history. Asking me what the spark would be to my generation's revolution.

I learned about it from you, because you are at the heart of all my fears and my softness. You are my spark. My first lesson in protecting what is innocent, and funny, and human.

I used to beat up the kids who called you retarded or crazy. I'd jump on their backs, bite the shit out of them, push their faces into the dirt until they bled the way you'd cried and I felt satiated. I believed my violence, exacted with love, could rectify some other's hate.

I think I never told you because I was afraid to watch you imagining me with some other kid's hair in my fist, both of us acting out of fear. Would you have wanted me beside you? Climbed down from the top bunk, up later than we should have been, imagining shapes in the shadows on the wall? Not an idea, but a you. A brother. A friend to be played with, to be laughed with, to be defended with steadfastness and joy.

After the election, we organized a rally and other people talked—about protest, gathering, voting. Inalienable rights.

BROTHER,

Blood and ink. Like you, like me, they were mad from the fear and silent from the shock.

They were champing at the bit of their boxes, the little government forms you have to check to see what oppression you've carried, and they were ready to fight and they were ready to cry.

I went on and on in this fury about wanting to spit on someone's feet or the terrifying rattle in my bones. I wish I'd had the courage to talk about you then.

The horror in my heart of how you might suffer for the impossible sin of being.

I don't know if I believe in my countrymen, but I know I believe in you. That your gentleness, your unwavering heart, your quiet feet, your full-bellied laugh, all those things in you that braid me to myself, might remind someone of their loveliest thing, and those sweet hearts, those undeserving children, left behind by our nation.

When you caught me, you crouched beside me on the floor and whispered, "What?"

But I couldn't tell you.

And so I reached for you and cried. I'd never grabbed you like that. You didn't know how to hold our bodies, but you held fiercely anyway. You were too thin. Like when you were born. You looked just the same. Your face little and pretty and blue.

Some people think it's the lack of oxygen at delivery, those moments in a noose, that give kids things like Aspergers.

I don't give a shit about that. I just give a shit about you.

Hanged at first breath.

Innocent.

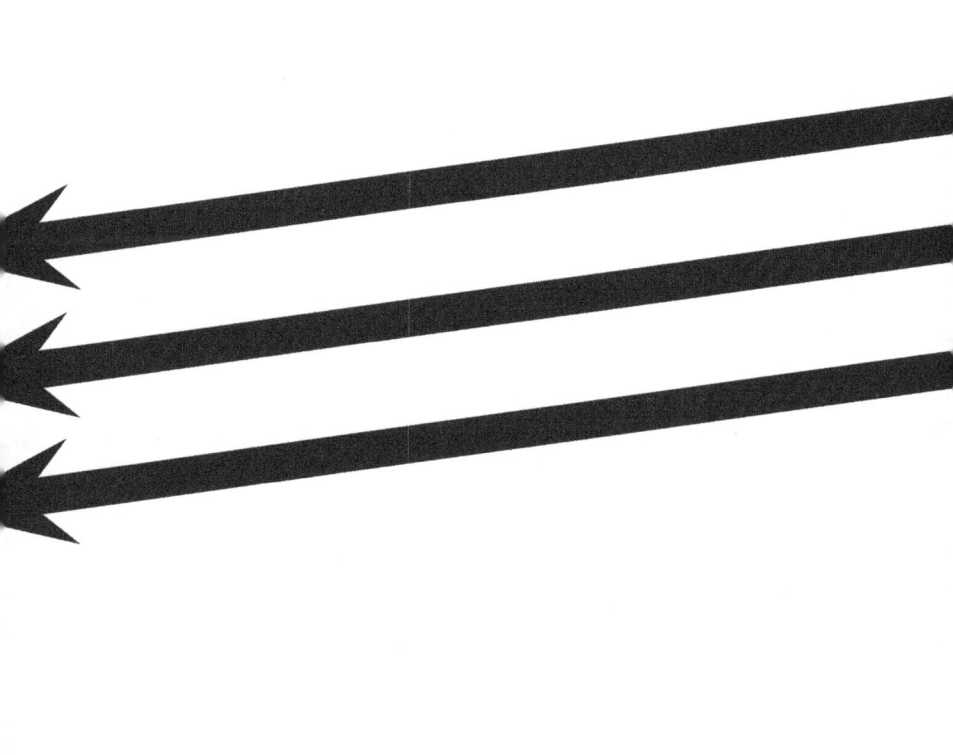

DRY LIGHTNING

by

M. J. Ridley

I HEARD ABOUT THE SCHOOL OF PEACE BURNING down after the car ride home. I had spent the late afternoon with my friend Tito, who was taking pictures of an abandoned factory for a school project. Well, we had thought it was abandoned. It took us about an hour to notice the cars moving in and out of the building's garage. There was even a convenient parking lot beside it that we could've gone to. Instead, we had parked by a field and walked around the perimeter of the area from a safe distance, fearing the possibility of some type of guard that sat around and waited for a chance to arrest any photography-enthusiast teenager that crossed their path.

The sky was a perfectly uninterrupted shade of icy blue. Sunlight cast a thin film of yellow-tinted white that glared off of building corners. The world wasn't moving the same way it normally did that day. It was quieter. As if, unbeknownst to the sky's sunny disposition, the tides had receded. Either that, or something more like an afterimage. I put my money on the latter. The sky didn't seem like something bound to crash. Instead, it lingered in its unbroken silence, like a pond after the ripples of a rock's plummet finally cease their motion. I was excited to head back home, to the warmth of the indoors. In the meantime, I watched the blue's quietness with the background chatter of Tito's camera clicking.

"I FEEL LIKE I AM BEING PROMOTED TOWARDS SUCCESS. I feel light! I feel the freedom of my spirit. Yes, now I feel free!" [...] "Filmmaking is art. And art can be a freedom for anyone." [...] "Freedom is...Friendship;" "Freedom is...Humanity;" "Freedom is... Education;" "Freedom is...ReFOCUS;" "Freedom is...Peace."
—"What Does Freedom Mean to You?" ReFOCUS Media Labs Students

The goal of ReFOCUS Media Labs is to teach refugees photography and filmmaking skills, giving them a competitive edge in the job market and a tool they can use to tell their stories. Even though Douglas Herman, the co-founder of the N.G.O., has received death threats for his continuously loud support, he shares everything he can on social media about the conditions of the refugee camp in Moria, Greece. He isn't safe there. Sometimes he's the one behind the camera. Other times his students send his videos about the conditions they experience daily.

The latest video on his social media was filmed by Herman

himself, and it began with the remnants of a poster. It showed facial expressions and the English words for them, but the only parts left intact were the faces for "angry" and "sad." Herman was sitting down in the middle of it all, this newly sprouted jungle of twisted metal bars and weakened roofs. He didn't mind the effect of ash on his clothing. He cast the camera back down again, to the poster's crayon-textured faces of children. Each face was allowed only one emotion. Some were invisible now. The poster was both a shadow of what the School of Peace had been and what it had become. His eyes lingered there. It was the day after the fire.

"THE ONLY PLACE WE HAD FUN AND COULD LEARN something. Now everything is gone."

"Our freedom is burned out!"
—Student quotes by @dfherman, Instagram, 03/08/2020.

The students aren't safe here either. People don't want to walk around the camp at night, fearing the possibility of being stabbed, or worse. Everyone was tense, having fled from the fires of war-torn countries to end up here, where a fire had happened just the other night. Their suspicions can't be confirmed, but everyone had a certain feeling about what had happened. The tensions between refugees and police had steadily risen. There had also been more altercations with what one article called "anti-migrant vigilantes." A different source called them

Nazis. White hands had crafted a hearth from hell while posing as God's angels. If they protested, riot police would smoke them out with tear gas. They were stuck.

APPARENTLY, THE REASON IT'S CALLED THE CORONAVIRUS is because there's a "corona," or halo, around the virion if you look closely enough under a microscope. The halo appearance comes from the crown-like spikes that surround their surface. When a halo of plasma surrounds the sun or some stars, that's called a corona too. But while the sun looks like a hazy ring of golden watercolor, the virus looks more like little white heads floating through murky black water. For some people, that's just what it felt like: these tiny, half-alive, angelic things spread their wings across oceans before anyone could process what was happening. People left for home, and didn't come back. Once everything moved online, the blackboards were abandoned too. I didn't want to leave. I was bitter to have lost the chance to see more "abandoned" buildings with my friends, and I was sad about accidentally leaving my favorite pillow in my quarantined dorm room. Everyone around the world was expected to do their part to help slow the spread of the virus. I was one of the lucky ones, and I know that a bit better now. I wasn't one of the people stuck waiting in a line to see whether death's white hands would show up or not. At the time, this is what I knew: if everyone stayed at home, washed their hands for thirty seconds with soap, and practiced social distancing, everything would be fine. All we had to do was keep to ourselves.

DOUGLAS HERMAN AND A NEWS REPORTER WALKED around the remains of the school together. He talked about what had happened. When he ran into other people who used to work here, they would hug and go back to picking through the charred remains of school supplies. This school had been a home for more than four thousand children. The N.G.O.s that ran the School of Peace posted a sign in front of the ashes: "We will rebuild the school. Together, light will triumph over darkness." A bit later, when the sun was beginning to set, the news reporter approached a man standing in the middle of what used to be his photography class. He was seeing it all for the first time. He cried. When Douglas approached, having already shed tears of his own, they high-fived. And then they hugged.

I'M HERE, BETWEEN THE SMOKE AND THE DIRT. I'M HERE, quiet and quiet. This is my fate. I am a refugee, looking for better life.
—"We are Refugee," ReFOCUS Media Labs Students.

There are swaths of unmarked graves for the refugees swallowed by ocean water in their attempt to find another place to live. For those that make it all the way to the Moria camp, there's little water to spare on washing hands. A limited amount of faucets are available, and the water is on for just a few hours each day. People wait in lines for hours to get truck-delivered food. Sometimes the food isn't edible and is thrown into the ever-growing border of trash heaps. The camp was built for three thousand people. Twenty thousand are there now.

Together, the refugees turn into bunches of clumped-up circles. Only small rings of light separate the gathering crowd waiting for their daily delivery of water. On some days a truck can come to bring a few bars of soap. There have been no confirmed cases of coronavirus within the camp, but if anyone does get infected, the virus would spread faster than lightning could strike. Asylum requests are further postponed because of the world's lockdown. People haven't stopped arriving. Their hands brush through the dry air, creating a static electricity that begs for some sort of release. There is not enough soap. There are not enough face masks. Even if the decrepit sinks could supply holy water, there couldn't be enough to put out any flame that picked Lesbos as its target.

IT IS GOOD THAT YOU GOT SICK MOTHER, I HOPE THAT they will give us vulnerability paper after a year, that we can go freely to Athens. I'm tired from Moria.
—"Lucky Vulnerables Series-02," ReFOCUS Media Labs.

I was surprised to see anything move in and out of that place, given the state it was in. All the building's windows were either boarded up or littered with holes. That was likely from people who, like us, saw the "abandoned" building and decided that throwing rocks was a good pastime. I bet they launched it over their heads, watched it soar, and then cheered with the satisfying sound of breaking glass pushed against concrete. One window was void of anything; no boards or glass—only an empty frame. It spoke louder than the loose bits of black asphalt that crackled beneath our feet.

It felt a bit silly now, us thinking someone was watching whenever we crawled under a hole in the fence or passed by a sign that said "POSITIVELY NO ADMITTANCE." The soft stains of rust that decorated the warning reminded me of the way icicles hang out of pipes in the winter, halted mid-flow. I watched Tito shiver slightly from the wind as he continued taking pictures of the building. I guess he decided it was still worth documenting, even though it wasn't technically abandoned. Although, it felt a bit more abandoned now than it did before. We didn't encounter any guards or fellow adventurous teens; only a few trucks driving out of a parking lot.

Now, our group stood silently amidst the open, gray space. The only one moving was Tito, my friend with the camera. I remembered him mentioning earlier that something happened in Lesbos, at the place he volunteered at. He helped teach refugees about photography. I knew that place meant a lot to him. He moved with intense purpose, and his mouth sat against his face like a gravestone. I made a mental note to ask him about it later. After fifteen minutes, we got in the car and drove back home.

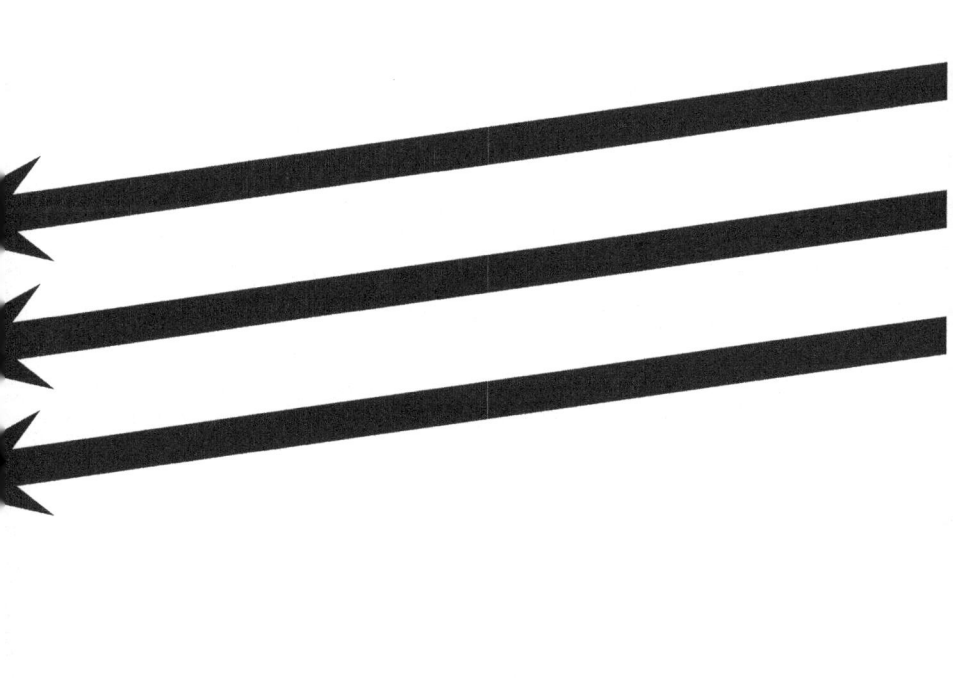

A PART OF THE CONVERSATION

by

Michael J Moore

THE MONROE CORRECTIONAL COMPLEX HERE IN Washington state was erected before Spanish influenza claimed more than fifty million lives worldwide. A walk within its living quarters gives the impression that its designers either knew little, or cared little about the prevention of infectious diseases among its occupants. Rows of forty cells—with bars, rather than doors—are stacked four tiers high, and a few feet from them stands a massive brick wall. The ventilation system is ancient, so the temperature inside usually matches that of outside.

After M.C.C. became the first prison in the state to have confirmed cases of COVID-19 among the incarcerated, I knew it was inevitable I would eventually contract it. Not merely because the structure is akin to a petri dish, promoting the rapid spread of every illness that finds its way in, but because prisoners have been dissuaded from reporting symptoms to such a degree that a civil rights attorney recently spoke on a local TV station about the conditions being imposed on my quarantined peers.

Then coughing began to ring out at night and during the day sick residents encouraged each other to stay in their cells, meanwhile, reporters quoted numbers from an Ohio state prison of "asymptomatic" carriers but never seem to factor in the lack of incentive for prisoners to report symptoms. These numbers were politicized, and used to make a case for states to ease restrictions, without anybody ever asking the incarcerated community for perspective on the topic. A few weeks ago, the projected U.S. coronavirus death rate went up to roughly 130,000 and I couldn't help but think maybe we should have been allowed to be a part of the conversation.

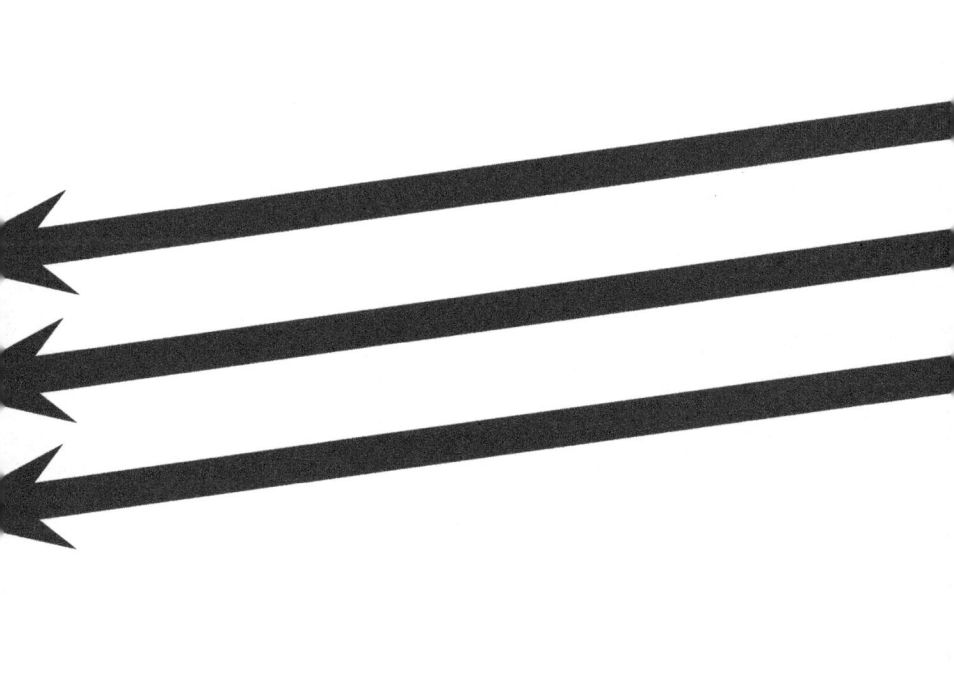

FICTION

GUIDE TO STRAIGHTENING

by

Emily Capers

| how to be more confident mixed girl 🔍 |

Top Ten HACKS for Better Confidence

https://www.teenmag.com/top-ten-HACKS-for-self-confidence/

Aug 12, 2018 - Having a bad day? Have the urge to hide your face underneath a paper bag? Don't worry girl, we got you with ten awesome hacks to boost your **confidence** today!

How to be More Confident: Makeup Tricks

https://www.beautygirls.com/how-to-be-more-confident-makeup-tricks/

Feb 20, 2019 - Whether you're highlight is on fleek or your blending game is a little weak, we'll show you how to clean up your look with 6 makeup tricks to build **confidence** instantly.

Learning to Boost your Child's Confidence

https://www.parentingboutique.com/learning-to-boost-your-childs-confidence

Sep 1, 2019 - You remember your days of puberty: changes to your body, **mixed** emotions, and low self-**confidence**. Remember working your way through these conflicts as you prepare to…

How Pretty are You? - QUIZ

https://www.tweenquizzies.com/how-pretty-are-you/

May 13, 2019 - Of course we know that looks aren't everything. Being **confident** is more than being pretty. So have some fun and take our quiz!

Guide to Straightening
https://www.mixedgirlbible.com/guide-to-straightening/
Oct 4, 2018 - Having a bad day? Have the urge to hide your face underneath a paper bag? Don't worry girl, we got you with ten awesome hacks to boost your **confidence** today!

Mixed Girl Bible:

Guide to Straightening

October 4, 2010

When you decide you want to fit in, you'll need to buy a flat iron. If you're too young for a job, beg your mom, grandma, anyone for about $150 because the expensive tools are the only ones that will get your hair as straight as the girls at school.

Don't bother with the safety instructions. You'll only see things like, "Keep this product out of the reach of children. Caution: Danger of burns." Or, "Not an effective solution to an identity crisis," and there will be plenty of time to learn about that later on.

You'll need to brush your hair before you begin. Your dry ends will break off, bent like spider legs, and collect in the bathroom sink. Wash those down the drain.

When the iron touches your hair, you'll hear sizzling. Hundreds of sparklers behind your ear, as if there's something to celebrate. As if you truly worked to burn generations of braids, of hold still, of shea butter, of afros, of Black power, of passing down stories on the front porch, of no I will not conform, at 450°F. What do you expect? That oughta make a sound.

Hours later, when you're finally done and checking yourself out in the mirror, you may be tempted to take the tool and clamp your nose in between the two hot irons, curious of what else you can change. Appearance is powerful. You've never looked more unlike yourself.

GUIDE TO STRAIGHTENING

If you're wearing this new look to school, be prepared for various reactions. Some people will be fascinated with your sudden change and may ask if they can pet you. Some will ask if it's a wig. Others will compliment you, saying, "I like your hair today." Today.

But no matter how cute you feel, do not pull out that dollar-store comb during class. With the first swipe and the first flip of your hair, someone will turn, point at you, and say, "Quit tryna act white." And, of course, with such a confident accusation, every neck in the room will crane and all eyes search for you, the imposter. They'll want to see you.

New Item!

Have beautiful hair in half the time...

"I'm not trying to act anything," you'll snap back while dropping the comb back into your bookbag.

"Alright, guys." The teacher will finally add. As if he had to wait for the right moment to interrupt. As if he, too, wanted to see your response to such a claim.

Class will continue. You'll try your best to only look forward, at the chalkboard, trying to focus on the teacher as he says, "Quit tryna act white. Quit tryna act white." Your classmates will nod and take notes.

You'll press your palms into your temples and feel sweat on your fingertips. You'll worry about how your hair looks. Gently, you'll feel around your hairline to see if your roots have reverted back to nappy even though your roots have been nappy this entire time.

Comments (5)

Leave a comment...

Jaime Miller

WE ARE ANTIFA

October 24th, 2010

Wonderful article!! i just recently bought my first flat iron (ah!) but i'm a little nervous because i read somewhere else that straightening your hair too much could cause damage and hair loss??

> **Claudia Smith**
> October 24th, 2010
>
> Thats true! It's called heat damage. Enough heat damage causes those fried ends to fall off bit by bit, until...
>
>> **Mariah Waters**
>> October 26th, 2010
>>
>> Yes, exactly. Too much heat (as in the hot tool is too hot or you're using the tool too frequently) will slowly alter your curl pattern. After three years of straightening my hair, it no longer curls :(Now when I wash my hair, I'm left with barely a wave.
>>
>>> **James Porting**
>>> October 29th, 2010
>>>
>>> Excuse my ignorance, but why would you put so much heat on your hair if it's so harmful?
>>>
>>>> **Claudia Smith**
>>>> October 30th, 2010
>>>>
>>>> Did you not read the article...... LOLLLLLL

Saige Turner
November 13th, 2010

If you damage your curls, is there a way to repair them?

> **Mariah Waters**
> November 20th, 2010
>
> Unfortunately, no. There are products and things that claim they can reverse and treat the damage but it's a gimmick. These companies are just trying to make more money off us. (What else is new?) The only way to truly repair the hair is to "big chop," where you cut off all of your damaged hair. For some people, that means shaving your whole head. That's what I had to do.
>
>> **Saige Turner**
>> November 21st, 2010
>>
>> Oh, okay. I mean, I think I would be okay with damaging my curls because honestly once I get a flat iron, I'll wear my hair straight like all the time, so it doesn't really matter to me.

GUIDE TO STRAIGHTENING

Mariah Waters

November 22nd, 2010

Yeah, I see what you're saying. But even above hair styles and hair texture, just don't forget YOU. Whether you're rocking wigs, straight hair, frizzy hair, no hair, you're rocking it! Love yourself through that entire journey. You know?

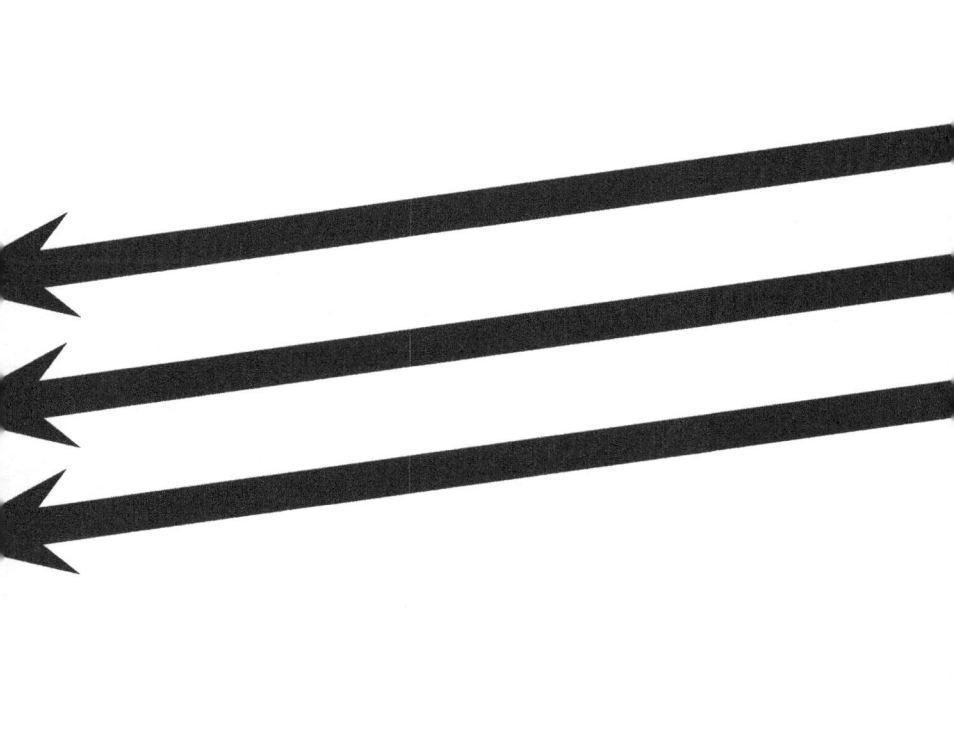

INTO THE WEEDS

by

Tim Jones

G.I. JOE PREPARED FOR WHAT WAS PROBABLY HIS tenth act of heroism so far that morning. The look on Joe's action-figure face, beneath the plastic helmet and real man's scruffy hair, was that ubiquitous smirk of cocky stoicism that said he knew he was about to get his ass kicked, but could take it. "Here I come you dirty Nazis," Joe growled in a voice sounding curiously like my boyish falsetto. Driving his jeep, rifle in hand, he would surprise the enemy with a daring leap over the chasm of cattails, mustard weed, pigweed, an empty Coke bottle, cigarette butts, and the trickle of fetid runoff that was the drainage ditch in front of my house. A summer sun, having just asserted itself over the pink, sleepy horizon, roused the dew that stained my knees. It was quiet in our neighborhood, as early mornings always were, except for the machine-gun pops and breathy explosions I created. Lustily, I thrust Joe toward the imagined Nazi camp, up a ramp of patted-down dirt, over the weeds and water.

    Gerald Ford was president that summer. Việt Nam, Watergate, and the scourge of dirty damned hippies had all recently passed like troublesome, overstayed boarders who had finally gotten the hint and slipped away in the night, though the small boy who was me by that ditch knew little of these things. The grown-ups, with names like Verne and Dot, and Dutch and Betty, who spent Friday nights at the V.F.W., and listened to baseball and Herb Alpert songs on A.M. radios, who knew right from wrong, had decided long ago that none of that would bother us much in our little town fifty miles outside Bigbad City.

    Joe tried, but crashed again, a tire striking the opposite bank, the jeep rolling, propelling his hard frame into the tall weeds. Stepping into the wet tangle to rescue the hero, I suddenly snapped from the righteous drama, alarmed by crunching gravel. The lazy morning sky became awash with red and blue flashes. I peeked through cattails at a rusty van, a squat tube perched on tiny tires, headlights bulging like the garish eyes of some corny vaudeville comedian, the body festooned with stickers. Policemen poured from a swarm of squad cars to surround it.

    They all stood tense for a while, until the chief pulled up and took stock, unhitching a nightstick from his belt. This seemed to mean something to the policemen, who began yelling for the van to empty. I marveled as people clambered out, like clowns it seemed to me, flopping from their tiny circus car. Beards and Fu Manchus. Unkempt hair the length of which

INTO THE WEEDS

I had rarely seen. Jesus sandals and biker boots. Ponchos and paisley. Dashikis. One wore a wristwatch on his ankle. "Freaks," my father would say, though my own knowledge of the label was informed solely by television.

I watched a chubby policeman take a baggie of green seeds from the jacket of the only Black man. "What we got here?" he smiled, grasping the man's halo of hair and slamming his skull against the van.

"Please man," the Black man grunted. "I'm a veteran."

"Yeah?" the policeman grinned. "Me too!" The other officers chuckled, then laughed hysterically when he drawled comically, "Guess that makes us *bruuuuh-thasss*, don't it?" He sliced his nightstick into the man's ribs with a sickening crack.

The chief pulled a bottle from the van, emptying its brown liquid onto the street. "Cuff 'em all," he said.

I crouched low in the weeds, feet soaked, watching them get shoved around, faces glancing off the van's side, hands twisted, clipped together. The chief grabbed one with cinnamon skin and two long braids, who looked like the Lone Ranger's sidekick, Tonto.

"What's all this, Walt?" I heard my father call from our porch.

The chief smiled warmly back at him, showing blocky white teeth, then swiftly drove his meaty fist into Tonto's stomach. He groaned, then crumpled. The chief beamed up at my father.

My father nodded to the chief solemnly, then, spotting me, stared with a fierce but almost forlorn look of fatalistic resignation. That brutal stare jarred me, confused me, and it would be years before I could decode it.

Understanding finally that this was not for little boys to see, that it was probably best to appear oblivious, I began searching for G.I. Joe. The hero was hard to find. The weeds were tall, thick, and thorny, their roots deep.

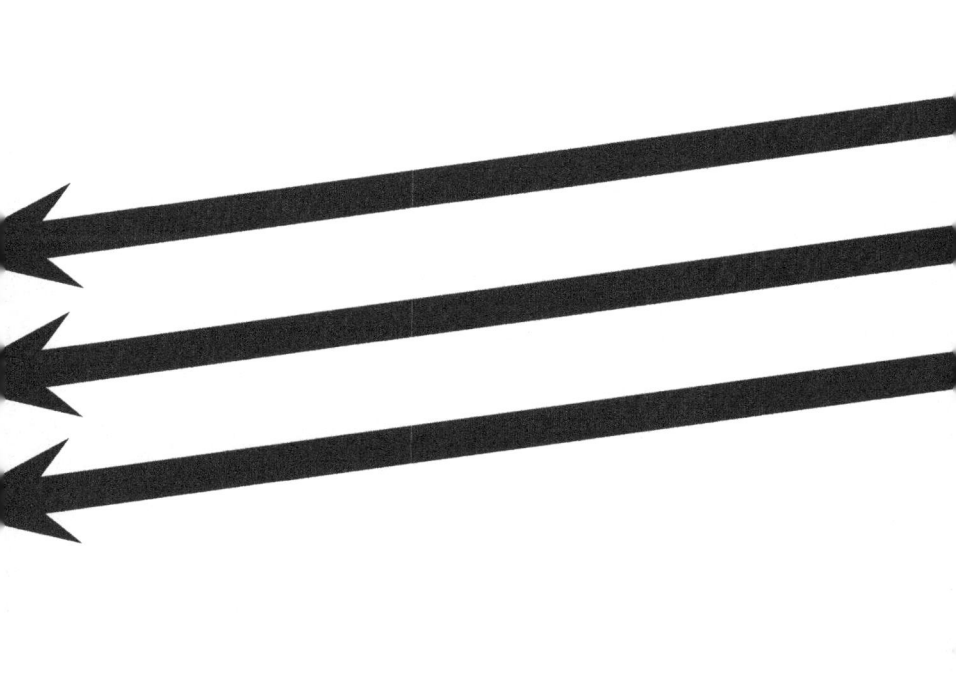

CHILDREN OF CHILDREN

by

Blake L. Bell

EYES OPEN, SHE ALMOST LOOKS ALIVE AGAIN. LAURA feels guilty for startling. An unknown illness, dementia-like, has kept her Maw Maw Elaine bedridden for years and sick since her forties. Laura's father settles his hand on her shoulder, as if to say, *Stay a while longer, look closer.*

She leans in toward a vacant face. She doesn't want to be, but Laura's terrified of this still body lying in a hospital bed in the lowest level of her paw paw's three-story house. She wants to ask, *If the machines keep her alive, is she, really?* but never does.

Her father tells her to say goodbye, so she pats a paper-doll-hand, says, "Goodbye, Savta," as Maw Maw Elaine's eyes, hard blue with yellow smoke clouding the pupil, amble to no perceptible logic.

AS SHE MATURES, HER FAMILY SAYS LAURA'S MEDIUM height and build, heterochromatic eyes, and curly brown hair match Maw Maw Elaine. Her father jokes that they all have "big Lithuanian faces," but some are taller, blonder. Genetics are a fickle kind of beauty, echoes of blood and bone.

THE OB/GYN'S LOBBY IS TOO STERILE. SHE FILLS OUT crisp white forms, holds her breath and checks the "Ashkenazi" box to test for genetic disorders.

Her older sister carries Gaucher disease but cannot have children. "It's OK," Molly says. "If you're a carrier, it's only a twenty five percent risk you'll pass it on, and you didn't marry a Jew, so."

Laura says she understands but wonders if, then why, numbers comfort anyone.

She hands the nurse filled-out forms, who asks, "Ashkenazi?" Then, "You don't look that Jewish."

If only she had a nickel.

She either looks too Jewish or not Jewish enough. "How does a person look like a religion?" Laura asks her father during freshman year of high school.

"They mean Eastern European," he corrects.

"You know you've got a Jew nose, right?" her boyfriend's friends ask her. One of them places his thumbnail against his nose and extends his pointer finger. She looks over to her boyfriend, stolen Natural Light spilling out the corners of his smile, and she laughs, too, but later, alone in her room, she measures from the base of her nostrils to the tip of her nose, then again from between her eyebrows. She researches plastic surgery, learns about correcting the shape of descendancy. "How cheap is your pops?" they'll ask, and she'll sit in silence. He does give her only twenty dollars to go to the mall.

Now, she fantasizes about telling those boys that big noses once meant power. That her father, more successful, more honest, than any of them would grow up to be, understood the dangers of consumerism, of conformity. She imagines telling the nurse to get out of her big Lithuanian face as she sits back down on cracked, pale-pink pleather and questions what it means to look or be like any one thing, what her child will look or be like. She hopes her child will look like everything, every possible thing. She hopes her child will be bolder than her.

SOON, HER INFANT DAUGHTER LOOKS UP AT HER with ice blue eyes. "She doesn't have them," she tells her father. "They're blue but not hers."

"Baby's eyes change," he says.

"Did mine?" she asks.

"No," he says, but Laura hears hope in how his voice lifts the O, as if his mother lives on in ovals, and if her daughter has them too, she'll live on and on, the life she deserved. One not stolen halfway through. One where she still sees her children, then their children, then maybe even theirs.

LAURA'S CHANGING ALICE'S DIAPER WHEN SHE SEES the yellow smoke, thin gold wisps enclosing the black of her daughter's pupils, once bright blue irises turning deeper lapis. She calls to her husband, "Joe! Come see. She's got them!"

She's here, she says only to herself and her cooing infant, spit bubbling. *We're all here.*

Alice blinks. When her eyes open, lineage yanks them onward, women bound by blood and pigment and shape, by melanin refusing to submit, to look or be like any one thing.

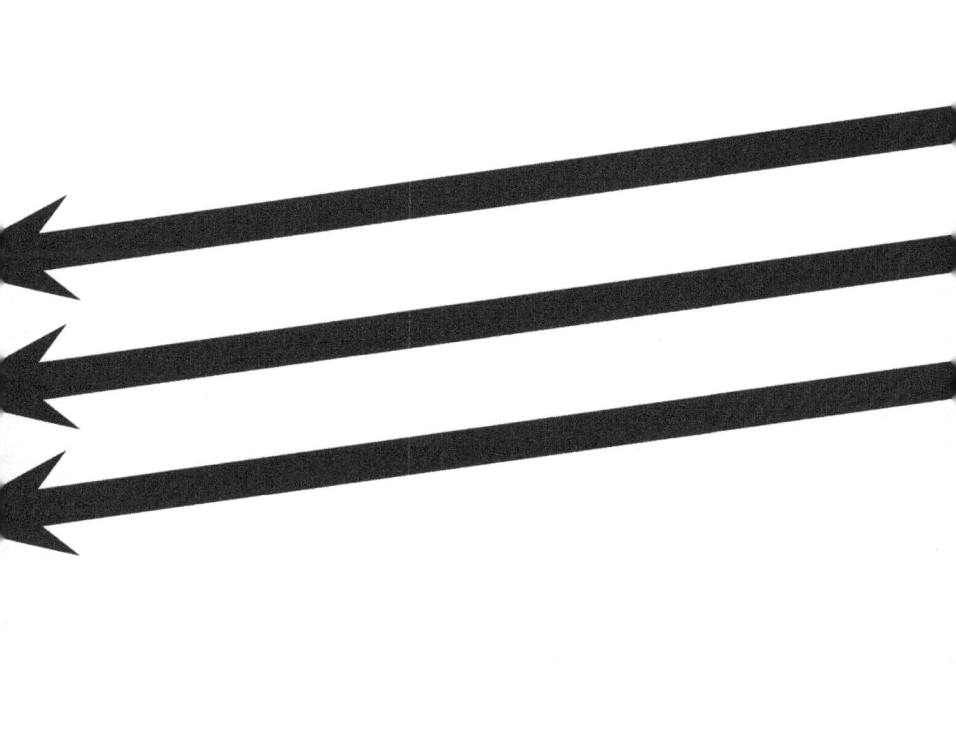

FROM THE MOUNTAIN

by

Priyanthini Guns

THEY FOUND HER HANGING FROM MY BRANCH.

The fruit's ripe enough to eat, said the officer, because that was the first thing he noticed. He picked one, smelled the skin, took a breath so deep the ripened scent of the sweet-turned-acrid juice filled his lungs.

Another untouchable. Don't touch it or you'll be cursed, said the officer beside Officer Fruit Sniffer. He wasn't referring to the fruit, of course. I've seen them patrol many times before, if not those two men, others with different numbers on their badges. I've heard their canvas trousers rubbing, their boots stomping, the sound of the clip, the bang before the scream— Get out of here you dirty terrorists, animals, shits of the earth! They were speaking to humans I had watched live generation to generation. I was a sapling when their elders made my lands their home. They were born people before they were stripped of their humanity. Their skin was made raw and bloody. Every few years ever since, more of them are pushed through into the dissipating jungle. As I lost my family, people grew in numbers. People came and people left and I don't always know where to.

IT MUST'VE BEEN PAST MIDNIGHT. IT USUALLY IS when the soldiers drink themselves to a stupider state for the state, only they won't admit it. The young woman's mother used to bring her at the end of summer when my fruit were ready for their favorite spices. I'd smell the roasting seeds rubbed in cinnamon rubbed in chilli. I'd hear the people of the village, sitting round the fire as it crackled. They'd laugh, sing and rest after a hard week of work. If they weren't in the field adjacent to me tilling what the men in branded caps call their "cash crop babies," they were taking the bus towards town to the "factory" where I don't see them for more than half the day. I wonder what it's like there. They come back dirty, their underarms smothered with an asafoetida-like stench masked with lavender and hibiscus. Their eyes tired, they walk up the hill past me as if already dead.

SINCE THE STATE SAID THE PEOPLE WERE "FREE," soldiers built barricades, guarded them and claimed all sorts of lies. Behind me is the Mountain of Minerals where the earth's riches rest between rocks and gravel. The soldiers echo the lie that it's the state's even though the people used to live there for centuries. They live on the outskirts now, on the edge of the earth against big guns, big names and no mercy. So, it was a little past midnight. It was the young woman's birthday. She said so when she met her lover and they held hands and kissed the night before while the village slept. She had said it was time. Her lover had asked what they'd do if they got caught. The young woman responded, If it wasn't them, it would be someone else, another soul, another body, another deemed "untouchable," worth less than an animal in the market at the most shitty market in town. They looked up at the stars through my branches, through my leaves. It's most beautiful under me, where from the cracks of my beauty another world shines revealing hope just under the celestials. In this bountiful vastness there is a tomorrow coming, birthing in just a day. The young woman said to her lover, If we don't fight for what's ours, no one will. Her lover held her. I heard them breathing. What I would do to hear their breaths again.

I RECOGNISED THE CLOTH THEY USED TO TIE HER FEET with. They tied the remaining silk onto my branch. They were a group of plain-clothed men. You could tell what they were about from a mile away—those trained by the state, for the state, unafraid to die for the state. They walked straight, with their chests out, their legs wide, their arms flailing in strict, succinct motions. One of them said, Don't make a sound. Another said, We did enough to her she wouldn't dare. They laughed. Those heartless beings laughed. This has happened before. The cracks on my trunk and on my branches reveal not my age, but all that I've seen. I cry on the inside and my tears carve the lines on my bark.

Her mother worked at the factory until the very second she died. The young woman cried that night telling me all about it. They didn't feed her mother, they didn't give her any breaks, they demanded production remain the same even as she aged. She was eighty-three-years-young and beaten when she went on strike. It took her one month to make a silk blanket, when it apparently should've taken a day. Her fingers were cut and deformed from years of working. She hadn't slept like a woman her age should sleep. They watched as she died on top of the silk. They stuffed it in her mouth and threw her on the streets. Then they packed the silk in a box and sent it across the world to a happy family for $89.99, more than the woman made in half a year.

The day after that the young woman's brother was taken from their home. The soldiers beat some of the other boys. They beat her too. They said, Don't touch me, untouchables, you dirty swine. I thought I'd never see him again, her brother. They took him and never brought him back. Her lover had come to comfort her. They said to the young woman, Look what I found. I stole it from a truck parked outside the factory. A whole box of the blankets just like the ones your mother sewed. I don't remember what happened, but as usual, the soldiers came, beat their bodies and took what wasn't theirs again. I do remember that the blanket was made of red silk. It smelled like roses and water from the river. The cloth they used to hang the young woman was soaked in blood, but was red before the blood dripped down its hems. I'm sure they chose it on purpose. Roses, river water, the scents of a young woman, her decaying flesh, and her dreams. Dying dreams smell like burnt plastic. A crow came and said he saw what they did to her. The young woman tried to take what was hers. She tried to do what any one would for their freedom, for their land, and for their sanity, but those bastards don't ever see it that way, do they?

AS IF IT COULDN'T GET WORSE. I SAW HIM. HER BROTHER. They brought him back, they beat him. They said, We can't touch your kind. Even though they do when they want something. They said, Take this dirty body and dump her in the water. It had been five years since he was taken. The poor boy shook, his eyes had seen things, his skin was tough and taut as leather. He had scars all over him. He took his sister and they were gone with the soldiers leading the way. They left as so many have.

The village functions as it has, and the soldiers patrol on, one by one. I see them and all they do, but I am a tree. I am burdened with the weight of seeing their evil and being too stuck in the ground to do anything about it. They are trying to get rid of us, too, in case we reveal all it is we have seen. Please, tell people about the young woman. Tell people about the Mountain of Minerals. Tell people about these evil men. They are taking what doesn't belong to them.

I AM THE WATER THAT FLOWS FROM THE RIVER which starts at the top of the Mountain of Minerals. I start with a drop of rain before I am the pool that keeps the bodies of those the state doesn't see as human. From the pinnacle and through the terrain, I feel every memory of every mineral, of every bone, of every drop of oil. This was a place for everyone and everything. I saw how quick man came to proclaim, This is Mine! I keep to my tracks through the earth, through the sky and down the back of the mountain. I watch the fish eat the flesh, eat the bones of the people. I see how they sleep in the cavities behind what were eyes. I cry and multiply. The circle of life brings forth life into a world where there is more oppression than there is freedom and those fighting for it lay here, in my bed, down my stream. I am a collector of tears, prayers and memories. They are building a factory near the mountain. As they build, my water turns murky. I used to be the kind of water one could drink in cupped hands by the banks. I am afraid that, like them, I am becoming poison. I don't want to die like those that I keep. I don't want to die. Something must happen or we are doomed. The state is killing us all.

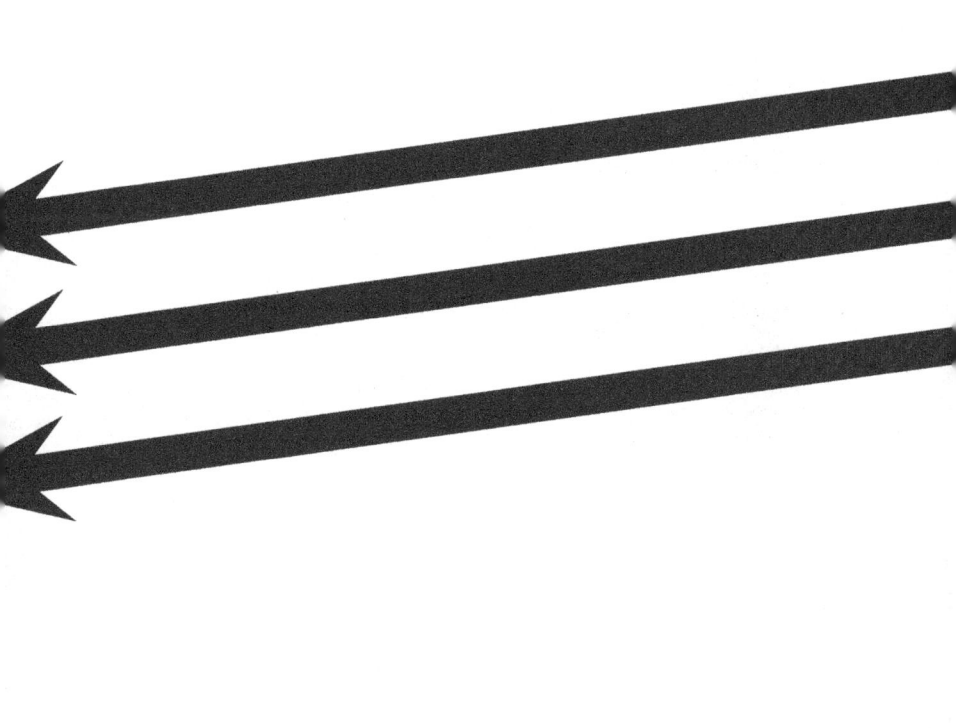

A POLICEMAN OF YOU

by

Daniel Nathan Horn

THEY MAKE A COP OUT OF YOU IF YOU AREN'T CAREFUL. They snatch you off the street, disappear you for a while, and then bring you back with a gun, a badge, and telescoping eyes.

Shit, it happened to Shaky just last week. I saw it happen, too—saw him get nicked. And off they roared in their black-and-white, tires spilling pale smoke on broken asphalt. I get a sick feeling thinking about the view out those windows. The blocks, they go by from rust to chrome, from indurate to neon. Ads go from gangland graffiti knots oozing from ashen brick and deserted overpasses to blinking billboards and corporate-person names writ large on skyscrapers. The city blocks are a slideshow, striae, a social fossil record.

Even the sky seems to change from steel-gray to the color of electric piss.

Here. Our homes have gone wavy with ruin, and we'll get

by. We'll get by so long as they don't come for us in the night and bring us back to our hoods as patrolmen with itchy fingers. We'll get by so long as our lost loved ones don't come back with telescoping eyes and radio chatter dribbling from idiot lips.

Here. There's a choker of Progress-with-a-capital-P around our projects, ever constricting. The gangs have re-aligned under One Broad Alliance, here where we fight wars just to see who gets to scoop the coyote roadkill from a gutter, maybe the only food in a three-block radius. All the while skyscrapers are gleaming all around, a claustrophobic horizon. And we'll get by.

Here it's O.B.A. against the cop-converts against everyone else: the not-gangs, the ones with brains still unscrambled and with non-telescoping eyes, those banded together for survival. Here we camp in landfills and desolate fields of automobile chassis stripped down to the frames, looking like an elephant graveyard. There in those shit-holes, those trenches of muck and mire, we'll get by so long as we don't get turned into police or get perforated by someone who has.

I saw Shaky just yesterday looking altogether un-normal, stalking perfect grids in the wrecked boulevards. Sure, he'll still say hello in passing. He'll even know your name, and he'll smile at you from behind his mirrored shades. But he never wore aviators, and he's never stood up very straight. You thought maybe he had scoliosis, actually. But worst of all, he doesn't go by Shaky anymore. His name is Jonathan. Jonathan Smith. And his hand always hovers near his hip.

To leave here—to be made a cop in their shiny labs, in their pristine polymer oasis—they make it seem like hitting the lottery. Free Lasik! Never need corrective specs again! But here—here in our ruin—we'll get by. We'll get by until they've made cops out of every one of us.

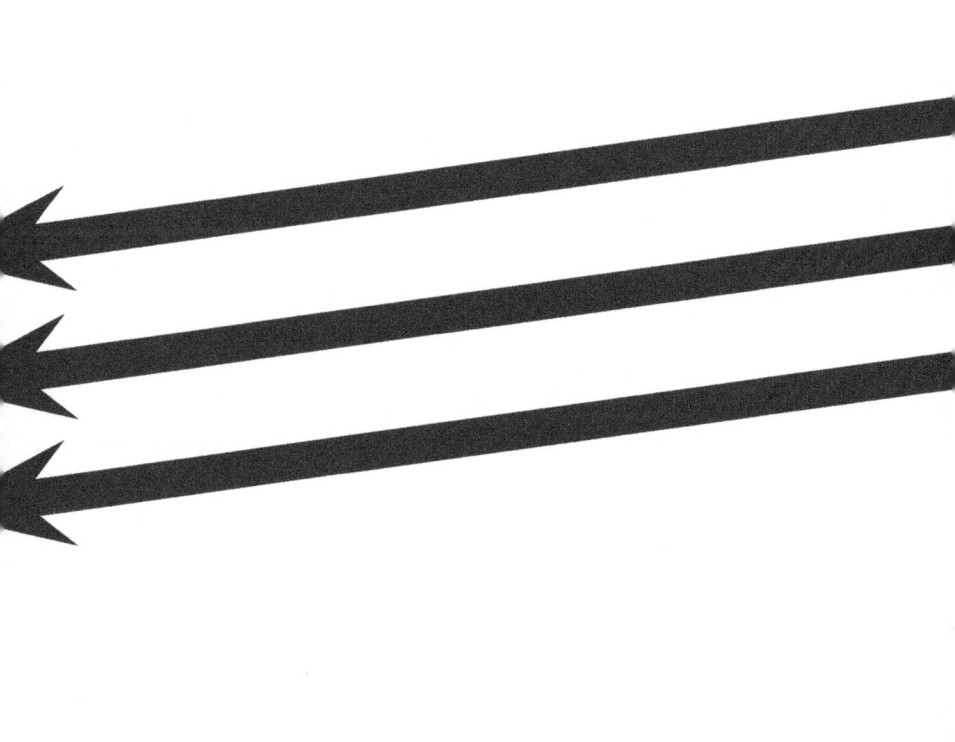

NOT RACIST OR ANYTHING, BUT...

by

Bill Wilkinson

"AGAIN," THE MAN GRUMBLED. HE PEERED AROUND the other passengers but couldn't see the protest out the windshield, just the rear of another bus. "Every damn day," he muttered, plopping back onto the sweaty plastic seat. Indecipherable chants floated through the open windows.

"I know," Rita said from two rows ahead. She twisted around the back of her seat and tossed the hair from her eyes.

"You know, they shouldn't be allowed to do this every day," he declared loud enough for every rider to hear.

Rita nodded. He's craving acknowledgment. She's heard his meek complaints before. She squeezed her small mouth into a grimace. "I know, right?" Rita called just as loud. "Don't these people work?"

He took the bait. "Why should I care what they're yelling about if all they're doing is pissing me off? There has to be a less rude way, right?"

"Amen," Rita said. "My name's Rita." An elderly African-American woman across the aisle glanced at them both before returning to her book.

"Greg."

"Someone's gotta speak up for the rest of us, right? All these others on the bus are probably fed up with the constant protests, too."

"They're just scared to say it!"

"Ha!" scoffed the woman across the aisle.

Rita smirked and seized the moment. "Feel like getting off here?" she asked.

"Oh, I don't want any part of those people," Greg said, flicking his wrist up towards the protest. He shook his head and slumped. "You can't speak to extremists. I don't engage with them. I'd get too pissed and start speaking truth to their bullshit. Then what do you think would happen?"

Rita nodded. Greg was perfect. "A viral video?"

"I like my job way too damn much to let some virtue-signaling social justice warrior fuck it up on Twitter."

"People are the worst."

"I'm just trying to get home from working all day, you know?" Greg whined. "Silly me, thinking if I play by the damn rules and go nine-to-five and pay my taxes and leave others alone I'd be left alone too. Silly me. I've gotta put up with this shit every day. These selfish rioters are just saying, 'Look at me! Look how woke I am!' I better shut up before the phones come out."

"I hear that," Rita said. "I was just thinking we could get

away from here since it'll be a while."

"Oh."

"I know a place we can go. Get off this stuffy bus and away from these sheep. Grab a drink." The old woman muttered something about Greg and farm animals.

"Lead the way," Greg said.

They hit the pavement to the sounds of singing and yelling. It was all so festive. "This way," Rita yelled and darted down an alley. Greg hustled after her, his dress shoes slapping the ground.

The real disruptions were months in the past. Most protesters were peaceful from the jump, but they were angry. A few opportunists busted windows and looted. A couch was torched in an intersection. Most just wanted to be heard. But stormtroopers rolled in with tear gas and rubber bullets, bashing skulls with batons. Eventually, things cooled. A few cops got fired, but others joined the nonviolent protests that have continued daily. It appeared a reckoning was underway.

Guys like Greg didn't get it. They never do. Guys like him ask, "How does this benefit me?" And when it doesn't, it's dismissed as a nuisance. Greg uses a good pump at the gym to deal with his frustrations and doesn't understand why everyone else can't do the same. His curls and bench presses were interrupted by the riots. His gym's front window was smashed and the place was trashed. "Fuck da Police" and "BLM" were sprayed over the walls.

That shit pissed him off. Didn't matter that surveillance footage proved the vandals were three white boys seen stumbling from a pick-up with a MAGA sticker on the bumper. If it weren't for the anti-police chumps, those three wouldn't have needed to act. And nobody can prove to a guy like Greg that Antifa didn't stage the whole thing with Soros footing the bill.

After four blocks of running, Rita slowed. She pretended not to notice Greg's raspy gasps. "This way," she said, hooking her arm around Greg's. She squeezed his biceps. She leaned in close as they strolled down an empty street lined with old brick buildings. She wanted him to think he was her protector.

"You know, I'm not racist or anything like that," he said as they walked through the strange neighborhood. The buildings had cracked windows and the sidewalks were crumbling. Greg doesn't come to places like this.

"Oh, no, of course not."

"I mean, I agree with some of what they're saying."

"Of course. Who doesn't?"

"But you know, it was just one bad apple. That cop should go to jail for sure, but that's no reason to destroy your neighborhood."

"For sure."

"There's better ways to protest."

"Yup."

"People just shout you down as racist if you say anything critical at all about those people."

"You can't even say anything so obviously correct as 'All Lives Matter,'" Rita said.

"Ha. I learned that lesson a while ago. But you know what I say? If you don't want the police to stop you, don't do anything wrong. Listen to them and they won't beat you. You know?"

"Have some personal responsibility."

"Damn straight."

"I like you Greg," Rita said, wrapping her arm around his waist and resting her head on his shoulder. He sniffed her hair and rested an exploratory hand on her waist. She suppressed a shudder and settled close.

"Where are you taking me?" he asked, replacing his rapid rambling speech with something more intimate. His hand slid above her waist, inching towards her bellybutton.

"Somewhere good."

"I should hope so," he said. "What are we going to do when we get there?"

"You'll see." She let his groping hand probe along her breast before wriggling free. She grabbed his hand and trotted down an alley.

Rita isn't the kind of girl Greg normally fantasizes about hooking up with. She's not like the girls in the videos he watches. Those ones have contours and attitude. They have puffy lips and pierced tits. They're feral, growling faster harder ooh like that oh fuck yes fuck me yeah daddy.

Skinny girls like Rita show up in the "nerd" or "housewife" or "petite amateur" or "librarian" categories. He rarely watches those, but perhaps she's a freak underneath. He was certain he'd find out because she so clearly wanted him.

She stopped in front of a black iron gate. Overgrown hedges along the fence choked the view. All he could see beyond was a sidewalk leading up to a door. "Is this your place?" he asked.

"This is our place," she said, reaching for the keypad above the gate's lock.

"Our place?"

"Yeah. It's a hangout. You'll like the guys here."

"Oh. There's other people here?" He couldn't mask his disappointment.

"What did you think?" she asked. "What did you think this was? You thought I was just going to pick some rando off the bus and take him home to fuck?" She glared and let him squirm. "Huh?" She relished this part each time.

"No, I—I don't know what I thought," he mumbled. "It's just—I don't know what I thought."

Rita giggled and grabbed his arm again. "I'm just fucking with you, Greg. I said I liked you, didn't I? I picked you, didn't I? I thought you'd want to meet some of these other guys, but we'll probably definitely end up banging one out."

"Oh," he stammered. "OK."

She rubbed his lower back and pinched a jellyroll. She punched in the code, a buzzer sounded, and she yanked the gate open.

They walked towards a brick building with boarded-up windows. "Is this an old school or something?" he asked. They negotiated several crumbling steps before reaching the door and another keypad.

Rita punched in the code and opened the door. "It was. Years ago little children came here to learn. Years ago when this neighborhood was very different. But we're taking it back."

Inside the building, a long, poorly-lit hallway lined with several closed doors extended to the far wall. Rita grasped Greg's hand and led him to the stairwell.

"Upstairs is where the action is."

Music and the babel of simultaneous conversations grew

louder as they climbed the stairs. "Sounds like a good crowd today," Rita said. She led Greg into an open room taking up the entire second floor. Against the near wall was a bar with liquor bottles lined up against a mirror and several occupied barstools fronting it. Men sat there deep in conversation and only the bartender glanced at the newcomers. Against the far side, men sat in low stuffed chairs. Men were gathered in little discussion groups everywhere.

"I love this song," Greg said when "Rockin' in the Free World" began.

"Want a drink?" Rita asked.

"Beer?" He nodded his head with the chorus.

"Coming right up. Make yourself comfortable."

Rita glided to the bar and he watched her lean into a guy sitting there. She placed her hand on his shoulder intimately and whispered something in his ear, her hair tickling his neck. Rita glanced at Greg before sitting on the bar and sliding across to the other side. She went on tiptoe to hug the bartender and then she disappeared through a door behind the bar.

Two dozen men scattered in groups of three or four, all dressed like they came from white-collar jobs like Greg, actively ignored him. There weren't any women. He waited awkwardly for Rita. Greg shuffled his feet, feigning nonchalance. He clasped his hands behind his back and studied the ceiling tiles. He pulled out his phone, pretending to study some text or email.

"Hey," a man called from the bar. Greg glanced up from his phone. "Hey," the man repeated. "What're you doing?" The man slid from his stool and strode towards Greg.

"Huh?"

"Who are you?" the man demanded, now standing a few feet from Greg.

"I'm Greg. I came with Rita?"

"And did Rita not inform you of our strict no-cell-phones policy?"

"Uh, no."

The man reached his hand out for the phone. "Welcome, Greg," he said sternly. "But we check our electronics at the door."

"I didn't know," Greg said, handing over his phone. Normally he'd be defiant, but he wasn't sure of himself here. The vibe seemed off. He may have made a mistake following Rita here.

The man turned off Greg's phone and pulled open a closet door next to the entrance and stored it in a basket with other devices. "The last thing we need is some spy recording us. We say whatever we want here, and sometimes people don't get that."

"Of course." He relaxed a bit.

"Anything else on your person that can make recordings? Tablet, tape recorder, anything?"

"No."

"Well, I trust Rita's judgment, so that's enough of the third degree. But you've seen what people do. They secretly record people like us just telling it like it is, and then the Twitter mob pounces and poof goes your job and family and life."

"I hate that," Greg agreed, his discomfort vanishing. "People are the worst."

"That they are."

The man Rita had caressed at the bar ambled over to join the conversation. He thrust a bottle of beer into Greg's hand. "It's like this, Greg. If I just happen to say, expressing my opinion as is my right here in America regardless of how crude or off-the-cuff or ill-advised it is—'I'm glad that ingrate of a protester, that snowflake little bitch, got smacked upside the head by one of our heroes in blue'—and someone records that and posts it on Instafuckface or whatever other place these people go to show how woke and progressive they are, then I'm done for. Right?"

"Right," Greg said, clinking bottles with his new comrade.

"And even if most right-thinking Americans would secretly, in the comfortable privacy of their own homes and minds, agree with that sentiment, the loudest voices will be those denouncing my bloodlust yet screaming for my head to roll!"

"Don't I know it," Greg agreed with a nod. "My bus home's been held up for, like, an hour every day for weeks by those people and I can't hardly say anything about it. It's just disgraceful. Un-American. I'm muzzled here in my country, you know? I popped off a little today. That's how I hooked-up with Rita. Luckily no jabronies had their phones out."

"And you, a productive responsible citizen just trying to return to hearth and home in what used to be called a 'free country,' who had nothing to do with anything, don't mean shit to them," a third guy said, bro-slapping Greg's back. "My granddaddy didn't smoke them Nazis just so we'd have to hold our damn tongues."

"Damn straight," Greg said. "God, I hated seeing that Saints quarterback shamed into giving, like, three separate apologies just for saying you shouldn't disrespect the military and our great flag. I mean, I'm not racist or anything, but you know, soldiers died for our freedom."

"Of course you aren't racist," the first jumped in.

"But people will assume that," said the third.

"It's just shameful," Greg concluded.

Another guy strolled up. "Buddy of mine was actually a victim of one of them videos."

"Shit."

"Goddamn."

"Motherfuck."

"Yeah, it was probably a whole set-up. I heard there's guys paying people to do that. They search out people they think they can nab, which is like totally racist prejudice profiling because it's always well-dressed white men or women that they get. Just shows you how racist the other side really is."

"What happened?" Greg asked. He finished his first beer and started another.

"He's always got to grab a quick lunch 'cause his job's super important and time is money and he just wanted his burrito bowl done right the first fucking time so he could scarf it down and get back to making money so his taxes can pay for all these lazy welfare fuckers to sit around smoking dope all day. But the motherfucking douche making it 'no habla,' of-goddamned-course, and he put the wrong kinda beans in it. So my buddy lays into him, but the fucking turd just plays all deaf and dumb and stands there like a fucktard. Some cocksucker bitch pulls out a phone and starts recording and all my buddy said was, 'Is it too much to ask in America that people learn fucking American?'"

"They want to be here, so fit in," the first guy said.

"And you can guess the rest. He gets fired, the company tweets some fucking statement about his actions don't reflect the views yada yada yada of the company yada yada yada, which is straight bullshit because all the guys at work told him it was bullshit. His cunt wife files divorce, and that's it. Blah blah blah, a guy's life is ruined cause some fucker can't do a menial job the right way."

Greg remembered this clip. Cancel culture sucks, but the guy in it, the "buddy," was way overboard. He had it coming. You just don't say things like that in public. But he quashed his doubts with two chugs from his third beer and nodded in agreement.

"So you can see why we don't allow phones," the first guy said, clapping Greg on the back and handing him a fourth glistening beer. The others melted into new conversations when Rita slid an arm around Greg's waist. "I see you've made some friends," she said. The first guy was still hanging around and Rita gestured towards him. "Roger is kind of the official welcoming committee. The rules guy. He keeps everyone in line."

"At your service," Roger said with a bow.

"So what is this place?" Greg asked. "God, it's refreshing to hear people speaking truth."

"It's just a place to hang out and be yourself without having to engage the P.C. crowd," Roger said.

"Everyone here," Rita said, sweeping her free arm around the room, "is just like you. They follow the rules. Have good jobs. They're responsible, patriotic Americans yearning to breathe free."

"None of us here are racist or anything," Roger assured Greg. "We aren't the oppressors or the haters. Those people out there marching and yelling and disrupting, they think all us white folk not with them are the problem. They lump us in with the Confederate flag-waving hicks and call us complicit, but we're just normal folks."

"We shouldn't have to put up with being yelled at by criminals in the street posing as protesters," Greg said.

"Precisely."

"We love America."

"Amen."

"We stand proudly for our flag."

"Support the troops!"

"Law and order!"

"Dammit, Greg! You fit right the fuck in here."

"And the music here is awesome," Greg declared as Kid Rock gave way to the third or fourth Limp Bizkit song since he'd arrived.

"I'm glad you like it," Rita said. She draped her arms around his neck and kissed him on the cheek.

Over the next hour, Rita shepherded Greg around the room, introducing him to small pockets of bitter men. Fresh beers kept appearing and Greg grew wobbly. The angry camaraderie freed his tongue and mind. He swayed gently when Rita, clutching his arm, showed him through a door behind the bar and introduced him to Marcus. This is where she'd disappeared to when they first arrived. She had to tell Marcus about her find. She knew Greg was perfect, but Marcus needed confirmation.

"Marcus," she said to a large bald man Greg hadn't seen all night. "Meet Greg. He's our freshest face." Marcus wore a brown military shirt over brown military slacks. A death's head patch was stitched onto the collar. Around his neck was tied a rebel flag bandanna. Greg willfully ignored the red armband. Marcus tilted his head and squinted at Greg for a quiet moment.

"Shit," Greg said, breaking the awkward silence. He forced a wry smile and a chuckle. "Now how in the hell didn't I notice you before?" Marcus remained quiet. His eyes narrowed and Greg's anxious laughter petered out. He looked to Rita for help, but she avoided his stare. "Nice to meet you," Greg said, extending his hand. Marcus let it hang wavering while he nodded and closed his eyes.

"Are you surprised about something?" he asked. He spoke just above a whisper. Greg leaned in expectantly so he wouldn't miss the next words.

"Pardon?" Greg asked.

"Surprised. Are you surprised?"

"Uh, no," Greg stammered.

"Does my appearance bother you? Offend you?"

"Huh? No, man. Free country, right? I've just been drinking and talking to everyone out there, and I just hadn't seen you yet."

Marcus reached out a huge hand and snatched the back of Greg's neck. The room spun and he just knew his head was about to be dribbled like a basketball. He tried wriggling free, but Marcus held him firm.

Then Marcus roared with laughter and pulled Greg's head all the way into his massive chest. He wrapped his other arm around Greg and patted his back, then stood him up straight. "Shit, I'm just fucking with you, man! That's just some initiation shit. Rita told me all about you, man. I had you going, huh? Fuck man, we bust balls. We're just a buncha mensches cutting it up. I wear this getup to get a rise outta folks. I'm not a racist or anything."

A weak trickle of stuttered laughs escaped Greg's mouth and he wiped sweat from his forehead. "Oh, OK, ha," he muttered. Rita wrapped a steadying arm around his waist and laid her head on his shoulder. "Be nice to Greg, Marcus," she cooed. "He's a good boy. Really innocent."

"Hey man," Marcus said. "It's great to meet you. We've got plans for you, boy."

"Oh, yeah?"

"Big plans. You got the look." Marcus stepped back and held his hands up like a frame. "That crisp FOX News haircut with the gel, all high and tight but not quite alt-right."

"Like a clean-cut businessman," Rita said.

"You could be on the school board. Or maybe the water authority. You could be a voice for us."

"Oh, I don't know," Greg said. "Really?"

"You look like the real deal, brother. An above-average Joe. Not Joe the Plumber or that pandering bullshit, but Joe the Assistant Regional Sales Manager of a modestly successful manufacturing outfit with between twenty-five and fifty employees that sponsors the local little league team. I bet you're a Rotarian or some shit. Anyhow, you look it. That's what people

NOT RACIST OR ANYTHING, BUT...

like. That's who they trust. You ain't some rich-ass elite trying to tell nobody how to think. No, you're Greg. You show up, play fair, and value peace and goddamn quiet. Am I close?"

Greg nodded.

"You look skeptical."

"No, no. It's a lot to take in. I've never thought about anything like that. I was just here having some beers, now this."

"Let me ask you. What's the greatest country in the history of the world?"

"The U.S.A. for sure," Greg said.

"Don't let anybody make you feel bad about saying that. All of us gotta look at ourselves and ask, 'What have I done to help this place that's given me everything?' You think burning buildings does that?"

"No."

"And sure, that cop murdered that guy. But he's just a bad apple. You pitch out the bad ones, you don't dump them all. Know what else I think?"

"What?"

"Guys like that cop are just bullies. He'd have choked out a white boy like you just as easily. It just is what it is, and some folk don't like to hear that truth. You don't think people are prejudiced when they look at me? Ha, they think I'm some dumb redneck who fucks his sister."

If Greg hadn't been so buzzed he might have sensed something was off. But Greg was swooning from the alcohol and the sense of outrage at the outrage of others. He liked being listened to no matter what he said. He liked hearing the truths the others shared. Greg knew Black people were treated differently in America and that some of the things the guys said were extreme. But he's a classic self-centered mediocre white man. He thinks he's doing enough by not being racist himself. By not using the N-word.

"The Black community's got their own mess to clean before yelling at us," Marcus continued. Greg nodded along, as he had all night. "Take a look at Chicago. Right? And their music. It's all bitch this, gold chain that. You know, my old man was dirt poor, didn't have nothing, he beat me and smacked my mother, but you don't hear me using that as no excuse for why I can't handle my own shit." Greg's nodding approval cemented Marcus's resolve.

GREG STARTLES AWAKE BENEATH A TOPPLED CHAIR. His legs are wet. He gasps for air. His tongue is plastered swollen to the roof of his mouth. He needs water. Rolling onto his stomach, he wretches and splatters black puke on the floor. Something clatters onto his back and he shimmies away from his mess, trying to free himself from the splintered wood.

His pants are drenched and he knows he pissed himself. But the liquid is red and he scrambles like a crab farther from where he'd been. Is it blood? Is he bleeding? It's dark and his vision is hazy, but he sees the entire room is trashed. None of the other men are around. Dim light shimmers where the plywood doesn't completely cover the windows.

He tries remembering. After meeting Marcus, the whole crowd sang "God Bless America." Marcus spoke to the crowd.

NOT RACIST OR ANYTHING, BUT...

Everyone began shouting and he grew frightened. Then he's reclining and Rita straddles him and leans closer and closer and closer, her mouth inching towards his, she's tugging at his belt but then it's all darkness and he's here, now.

He runs his hand down his pants but can't tell if he's wounded. He bends his legs and staggers to his feet. His only pain throbs at his temples so the blood must not be his. He's in jeans, not the slacks he'd worn there from work. And a torn flannel shirt. "What the fuck?" he croaks. The clothes aren't his. He wobbles on unsteady legs. "What the fuck?" he says louder.

Blood streaks the wall in front of him. The chairs and tables are toppled. Someone took an ax to the bar. On the wall are Black Lives Matter banners that hadn't been there before. They're torn and marked with swastikas and "KKK" in blood. Is it blood or is it paint? There's a can of overturned red paint in the corner. Graffiti is scrawled everywhere. "WHITE LIVES MATTER" and "MAGA." A noose hanging from a light.

Greg rustles through the rubble searching for his clothes. He yanks the closet door open where his phone had been stored, but it's empty. Get the fuck out. Get the fuck out.

He flees down the stairs and flings the door open. The early sun is just above the treetops. The street is empty but he hesitates. He looks horrible. Terrifying. He doesn't have his phone or wallet. He doesn't know where he is. He can't possibly ride the bus. It's Thursday and he has an important meeting at ten. He can't fuck it up or he'll lose his job.

He takes a step on the walkway and hears, "Freeze, goddammit! On the fucking ground!" He can't see who gave the command. His face is slammed into the concrete from behind.

A heavy knee crunches his back, forcing all the air from his lungs. Before he can suck in another breath, a knee pins his neck.

"Police, asshole," the voice whispers in his ear. "How's it fucking feel?"

Greg can't answer. Boots clomp in front of his eyes. All the legs are protected with shin guards like a catcher's and long black truncheons dangle from unseen arms.

"Quit resisting, motherfucker," another voice yells. Both voices are familiar.

"You're under arrest," says the first. Greg can't breathe and he can't protect himself. He can't protest his innocence or ask what they think he did. He's helpless. Greg's left arm is wrenched behind his back by the man choking him. Another person grabs his right and jerks it around to cuff him. He can't breathe. His face is mashed into the concrete. Then he's pulled to his knees and something pops in his back and pain radiates his body and he gasps for oxygen.

"Ahhhhh!" he screams.

"Shut the fuck up!" someone yells and slams the back of his legs with a baton.

"Help!" he manages to shout. He can't see that it's Marcus holding him upright while Rita spears him in the sternum and Roger slugs his jaw.

When his eyes open next, he's tied standing to a pole in a low-ceilinged room. "Help!" he screams. "Goddammit somebody help!"

Marcus, Roger and Rita file through the door in riot gear with POLICE in white letters across the front. "He's awake,"

NOT RACIST OR ANYTHING, BUT...

Roger declares. "I didn't think I hit him that hard."

"I didn't do anything," Greg yells. "This isn't fair!"

"We know," Marcus says quietly.

"What?" Greg asks. "You guys are cops?"

"You love the police!" Rita taunts. "Isn't that what you said? Don't do anything and they won't bother you? Don't resist and they won't beat you?"

"We know you didn't do anything," Marcus says calmly. "But the video might lead others to draw vastly different conclusions."

"What?" Greg stammers. "What video? I know my rights. I want my lawyer. Where am I? What precinct?"

"Oh, we aren't cops," Marcus chuckles.

"What the fuck is this?"

"Didn't feel good, did it?" Marcus asks.

"Huh?"

"The knee to your neck."

"I didn't do anything."

"So?" Rita spits.

"Don't forget the video," Roger adds.

"What do you want?" Greg demands.

"Nothing," Marcus says.

"Nothing?"

"Nope."

"Why me?" Greg whimpers. "What did I ever do to any of you?"

"Why not you?" Rita hisses. "What makes you so special? I've been listening to you on that bus for so long. Bitching and moaning about how unfair it all is. Boo-hoo, you entitled prick.

That's why you."

"We listened to what you said," Roger says.

"And you agreed with some messed-up shit," adds Marcus.

"Those were just words," Greg mutters. "They don't mean anything. I've never done anything to anyone."

"Just words?" Marcus scoffs.

"Fucking coward," Rita shouts.

"I'm not racist. I've never hurt anyone."

"Words matter," Rita says. "They have consequences."

"So what? Are you blackmailing me? You want money? Are you going to turn me in? Make me the next viral star? Am I canceled?"

"No," Marcus says.

"No?"

"No."

"Then what?"

"Maybe you'll learn something. Maybe you won't only think about yourself. If nothing else, maybe you'll learn to watch your fucking mouth," Rita suggests as Marcus removes the handcuffs and the ropes. Greg slumps to the floor and watches Marcus and Roger leave. Rita kneels down beside Greg and grabs his crotch. "Like I'd ever fuck someone like you," she whispers before getting up and leaving him crumpled on the floor cradling his balls.

"Oh," she says, tossing a thumb drive at his face. "You may want to see what you're capable of."

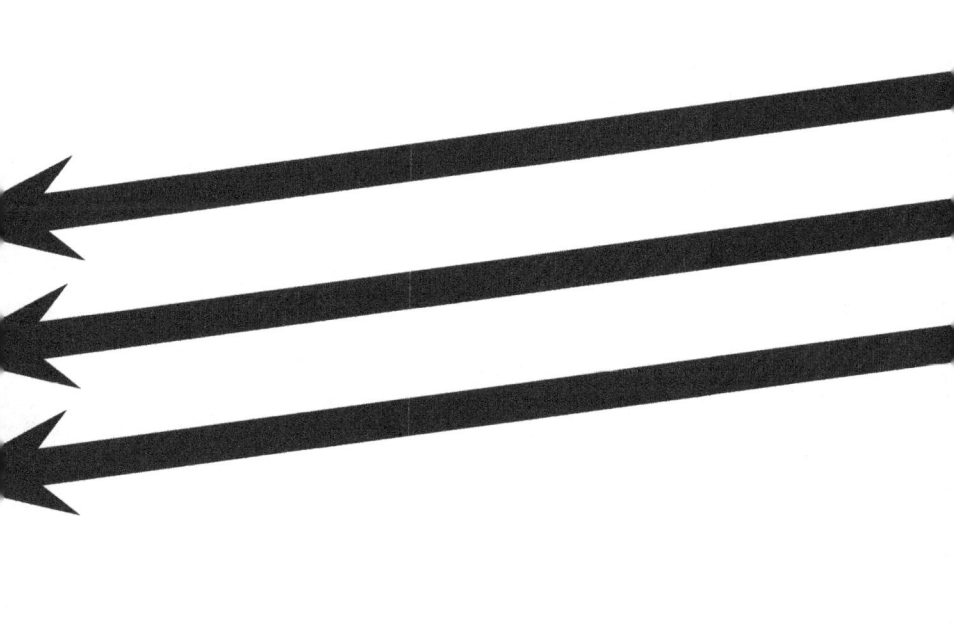

A REASONABLE FASCIST

by

Matt Harris

HE WAS A REASONABLE FASCIST, BAKING IN THE brutal sunshine in the centre of his cage. He was standing before a microphone on a makeshift stage, his followers were crowded in the square before him, and the whole gathering was circumscribed by temporary metal fencing, there to keep the fascists in and their enemies out.

The rally had been organised by a loose confederation of far-right groups, including remnants of the English Defence League (once headline news but losing relevance by this point), a new anti-Islam organisation and a number of smaller groups. There were hundreds in attendance, perhaps close to a thousand. The city had allowed them to stage the rally in the centre of Piccadilly Gardens, a busy square in the centre of Manchester, but they had fenced off the area and funnelled the fascists into it with horses and riot police, then closed them in. A few thousand protesters were there to condemn the rally, all gathered around the fences looking in, and I was with that number. Thousands more people were passing as they shopped or took their leisure, looking over with curiosity or indifference. It was a blazing hot Saturday afternoon.

The attendees of the rally were all white and all men. I couldn't see a single woman in there. The men mostly had shaven heads. Within their cage a party atmosphere prevailed. The turnout was good, the weather was good, they had an audience and they had alcohol. Every man clutched a can or two of beer, and from their drunkenness it seemed that most had been drinking for hours before they arrived here.

On the stage, the reasonable fascist presented a different aspect. He was a slightly overweight, middle-aged white man with a neat, unremarkable haircut, and he wore a grey suit. Behind him stood three other men, one of whom was Asian and wore a turban. He was the only brown face within the cage. He was quite old and he wore a blue T-shirt decorated with the slogan "STOP MUSLIMS RAPING DAUGHTERS."

The reasonable man was giving a speech.

—We are not racists! he said. We are not a racist or prejudiced organisation! We are a modern, tolerant, multiracial organisation that wants to protect our families!

Very few of the men in the audience were listening to him. Most were talking, laughing, shouting. Many had their backs to him. Carrier bags full of beers were being passed around, songs were being sung. Outside the fences a few protestors were shouting things, but not with much enthusiasm, for the rally's disposition was ludicrous rather than antagonising. A crowd of drunk and happy bald men locked in a cage, ignoring a speech, while protestors looked on them like zoo visitors and vast crowds of heedless shoppers streamed past with Primark bags.

—All we ask is that our British values are protected, that our sons and daughters are kept safe from abuse and indoctrination. We support the ordinary working men and women of Britain, who are so often forgotten by our politicians. We are not prejudiced! We are the voice of ordinary, reasonable British people!

—Sieg Heil! shouted a man in the crowd.

He performed a Nazi salute in the direction of the stage, and several of his friends joined him.

—Sieg Heil! Sieg Heil!

The sound of idle, placid conversation morphed into excited chatter as the men all took notice of the Sieg Heiling. It caught on at once. More and more of them joined in with the shouting and saluting, arms striking out with vigor and fury. For the first time the rally seemed to take a certain shape, to develop some purpose.

The man on stage was dismayed. He tried to press on with his speech for a few seconds, then fell to admonishing his audience.

—Stop that! he said. That's only going to make us look bad! Stop it! This is what they'll show on the news you know, this is the message the media will put out.

But his audience didn't care about the media's message, and they weren't listening to him. They were transported, joyful. Who among them would ever have dared to make that forbidden salute while standing alone? Only the most reckless. And yet now they Sieg Heiled together with impunity, gleefully transgressing, flaunting their strength in union. They were all transformed. They shared in the ecstasy of fellow-feeling, the bliss of mob fury. Each of them was among men like himself, united against a common enemy: the outsider. Together they were something unstoppable, and although many of their faces showed anger as they saluted, more of them showed joy. Susan Sontag called it "the dissolution of alienation in ecstatic feelings of community," and considered it one of the vital ingredients of Nazism.

On stage, the reasonable fascist was alone. In the pit below him his followers were indulging in the true ecstasy of fascism. They were ruining all his careful work for the cause and they were having a wonderful time doing it. He did not fit in. Had he ever? Maybe he was once one of the boys, but his rise to prominence had isolated him from the foot soldiers. More likely he had always been an outlier. I imagined him at the far-right get-togethers of his youth, enjoying the fury and the beautiful hatred but concerned that it was going nowhere.

Shall we talk strategy, lads?
I've just finished Mein Kampf, does anyone want to borrow it?
Maybe we should keep sober during meetings?

That practicality, that immanence of mind, had made the man a leader—but it had also made him an outsider, the thing most loathsome to his own movement. Perhaps that is the fate of all fascist leaders. The followers need the leader, for it is he who calls the rally, leads the putsch, embodies the state; they will worship him, but in their hearts they will also despise him, for he is not like them, and the soul of fascism is to despise those who are different, and to seek a sublime totality with those who are the same.

Inside the cage the men reveled in the fiery discharge of mass anger, drunk on the awesome transcendent power of unity, each one of them a white man among white men dressed similarly, similarly furious, chanting the same words and making the same forbidden salute. A glorious abnegation of the self.

...while the reasonable fascist stood on stage and worried about public opinion, and about the way his rally would look on the local news. The men behind him on the stage had moved away to confer. Beyond the fences the protestors were energised by the Sieg Heiling, and a rousing chant of *Fuck off Nazis!* had risen up. The journalists present were hungrily training their lenses on the drunken morass of saluting fascists. On stage their reasonable leader had given up appealing to his audience and was simply standing there, lost and desperate, his face red and his clothes heavy with sweat. I have never seen a lonelier man.

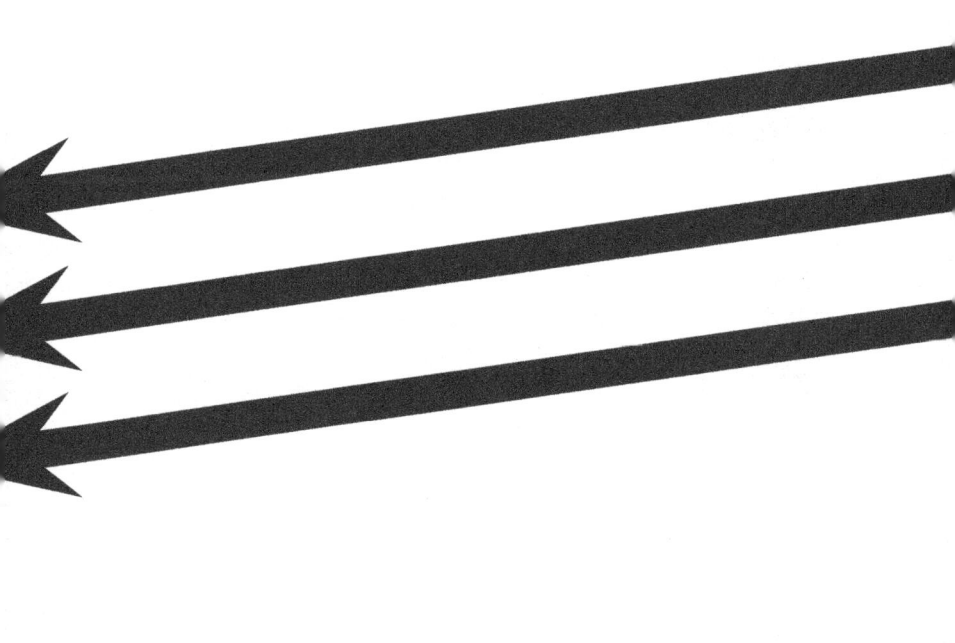

HEADLESS AND HANDS

by

Josh Wagner

RUNNING LATE SO YOU TAKE THE BYPASS, AND THAT'S where the red and blues ghost up from behind. Here we go. Ease off and lean to the right like steering a bicycle. Hazards on. Kill the engine.

Now comes the longest part. For the next thirty seconds trains of thought cram and collide. Not so much whether or not you remembered to replace the old expired insurance card with the new one they sent three weeks ago, or how much your premium might spike when it rolls over; but mostly visions of dark red streaks on the upholstery and whether or not you'll still be breathing ten minutes from now. It radiates in tremors down your arms and across the backs of your hands. Hands. Where do I put my hands? On the wheel, knuckles tight? Too threatening. In your lap? Hell no. Sound of a door. In the rearview, a blocky headless torso. Your window's still up, but don't be on the button as he walks over because that will occlude your hand in the shadow of the door. You don't wonder whether Krystal will be pissed because you're late again, but how she'll manage to hold it together in front of the kids, and if she does break down and start to cry will her father finally reach out? License, registration, insurance—should have had it all ready to go. They don't like having to ask. Too late now. Anything beats reaching. And that loud metallic click of the glove box hatch. Oh well. Too late. Hands on the wheel. Don't grip, don't grab. Relax, act natural.

Well past the back bumper, nearly to the window—which you tried but only got halfway down before jerking your hand back on the wheel—asking yourself if there are any drugs or weapons in the car, even though you have never had anything even resembling a weapon in this car, *ever*, and the last time you lit up was graduation. But are there, though? It's like your brain refuses to be absolutely sure. In the glove box? Is that why you won't open it?

"Good evening, sir."

"Hello." Was your tone submissive? You consider the shape of your mouth. Fine line between smile and grimace. Relax. Compliant. Like pliancy. Easy breezy. Chill. Chill. Chill. Anxiety will often manifest in behaviors mistaken for guilt or aggression.

"Do you know why I pulled you over?"

"Speeding?"

"Were you speeding, sir?"

"Was I?"

"Were you?"

"I don't...No. Maybe."

"You've got a taillight out on the right side."

That happens. A thing that happens. Lights just go out. No one knows why.

"License and registration, please."

Don't reach. Don't grab.

"In the glove box."

There's a way to squeeze the button so it doesn't make that clicking sound. OK, yeah. Definitely should've done this before. What a mess. Gonna have to dig.

"How's your night so far?"

"Fine, Officer. Good."

Like how dentists chat you up as they assemble a nightmare scaffold inside your face. Do you have any drugs or weapons in the car? Are you affiliated with gangs? Any bodies in the trunk? There. Shit. It's the old one.

"New one's in here somewhere."

"How about your driver's license?"

Yeah, of course. But not in the back pocket. Gives you a cramp to sit on it.

"It's in my jacket. On the floor."

"Go ahead and get it out for me."

Still strapped in, you shift your core until your entire body kind of tremors leaning over. Nerves.

"Have you been drinking tonight?"

"No sir, no drinking."

Just reach in and pull out the wallet. A natural motion. Happens all the time. Do you have any weapons or drugs in the wallet? There, it's out. Leave the jacket on the floor. Still breathing. Deep breaths. Not too deep. No shots fired. Click. Pocket pen light. Blinding, blotting out his face. Headless. Collar stiff. Strong, calloused fingers. Plain wedding band. You glance at his sidearm. Where are my hands? Insurance. Still need to. Don't lunge. Glove box hangs open like a coffin.

 Maybe ask again? Is it OK if I—

When the officer leans down, you have to physically will yourself not to jump, but since the reaction is autonomic the very act of restraint upgrades the jump to a lurch. Freeze. Breathe. Still breathing. Just looking at my face, comparing it with the photo. Normal. Random impulse to run out of the car, or turn the key and floor it, drive into a wall or through a guard rail. Dodge a bullet. Stay alive. Should've taken the freeway. Tell him you have a gun. You don't, though. Never even touched one. You disarmed that man who was threatening Krystal with a knife. Drunk at the club. Stepped up and took it from his hand like snatching keys off the counter. No fear then. Confidence of love. Now you're wondering if you have any warrants out when you've never received so much as a parking violation. Unearthing the bracken of memory for something to confess.

 "Please stay in the car, sir."

 Now he'll run your name against a confederacy of databases for classification and authority. Name: Man. Age: Aggression. Height: Suspicious. Never did find that registration. Clear shot through the back window's defrost lines. Always facing away. Don't reach, don't move. Breathe. Wait. Maybe he'll come back with just a warning, have a nice night. Hands on the wheel. No, *on* the wheel. Is that a weapon? No, this a steering wheel. Sir, step out of the car, but keep your hands on the wheel. How do

HEADLESS AND HANDS

I? Are you resisting? Shots fired. Flash flash, the red and blues. Hypnotic. A lullaby. Stop. Relax. When this is over, you'll drive up the road then pull over again and call her. I love you. Door opens. Headless. Lights in a casino whirl. Where are his hands

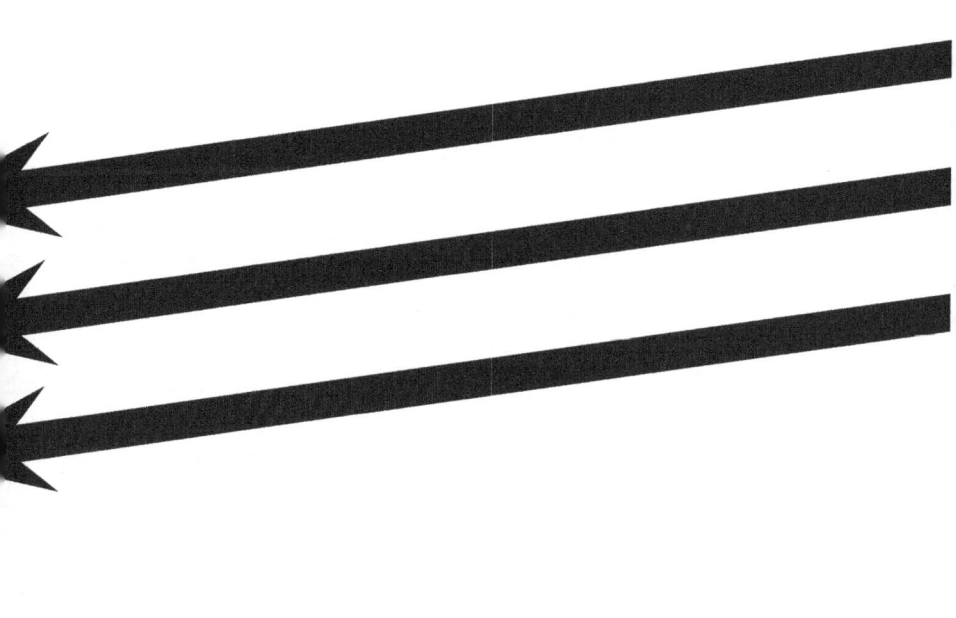

THE PHILANTHROPIST

by

Sam Palmer

<u>1680-1692</u>

THE SHIPS SAIL THE OCEAN, THEIR ROUTE A NEVER-ending triangle. Inside, below, they are hot and steamy with stolen breaths and screams.

When they reach their destinations, they are slick with blood and excrement. Full on departure, quarter-empty by the time they arrive. The man calls this wastage. It is planned for, acceptable.

Sometimes, in moments of reflection, the coins in his pocket feel sticky with the sweat of forced labor in another land. But the metal wins. It always does. The weight of it smooths out any wrinkles of guilt.

1721

THE MAN DIED TODAY. HIS NAME IS WELL-KNOWN. It is written on the city, painted in money. He was a good man, they say. A Christian. A philanthropist.

2020

DISEASE IS IN THE AIR. SO IS HATRED. PEOPLE ARE ANGRY. A killing, unlawful, has become a shockwave eating up ground and water as it travels the world.

The man's statue watches it all with its molded ponderous face as it stands in the centre of the city. A bronze malignancy.

Masked and holding placards the people cheer as ropes pull it down. Four tugs. It doesn't seem enough for something which has been standing for so long, but it is. Change can come easily when it is wanted.

People roll the statue to the harbor. It makes a muted *flump* sound as it hits the water and rapidly sinks.

It's vandalism, someone says.

They don't know that people can be vandalized too, hearts, bodies. That they can have another's wants and needs tattooed on them.

It's in the past, someone says.

They don't realize that history is the future. Inequalities and prejudices come around again like fringes and flares.

The man's name will be forgotten soon. The ghosts are glad, but they don't sleep. There are many more to go.

THE BRIDGE

by

Lin Lucas

ST. LOUIS, MISSOURI
July 5, 1917

Oureka Daring stood on the gravel road in front of the municipal quarters where she and a thousand other refugees were being warehoused. The midday sun stung her cheek like a backhand slap as she stood hunched in the last cue of folks all preparing to make the first exploratory journey back to East St. Louis. A hawk-faced man from the Red Cross checked their names off a list before they climbed up into the crowded flatbed trucks that would ferry them back. The National Guardsmen who would accompany them stood alongside the trucks, rifles slung over broad shoulders.

Oureka wondered whether any of the soldiers had been among the troops who had passively observed the carnage three days before. She had heard tearful accounts of soldiers watching as colored women and children were dragged from streetcars, beaten; of men, stomped, clubbed, tortured by roving bands armed with whatever they could find to inflict suffering. Survivors told of guardsmen passively observing as homes were set ablaze to drive the terrified occupants out into the waiting arms of the rampaging mobs. All the child knew for certain was that none of them had come to her aid as she stood screaming her throat raw, pushed along like flotsam by the tide of fleeing Black bodies, all the while looking over her shoulder, a forlorn hand reaching back towards her father.

"Let me help you," a petite honey-complexioned woman said as the girl attempted to pull herself up into a crowded flatbed. The woman's dark hair was wound into a neat chignon that adorned her head like a crown. Her white blouse was pristine, and the gray skirt bore no traces of the ordeal that had brought them all there. The woman extended a patient hand.

Oureka studied the manicured nails of the proffered hand, met the stranger's gaze with proud eyes, then turned away. Placing her hands on the bed of the truck, she hopped aboard. The manicured woman smiled, climbing in after her. A moment later, the truck engine cut the afternoon silence. The huddled passengers lurched forward as the vehicle sped away in a cloud of dust.

Three days after the riot, Oureka still stank of fear. She was unkempt; her long nappy locks were matted with dust and ash. Dressed in dungarees and a red-and-white checkered shirt, she looked like a boy but for her delicate chin and wide almond-shaped eyes.

THE BRIDGE

Precariously perched on the edge of the truck, Oureka hugged herself against an inner chill that no amount of sunlight could soothe. A thin vertical scar below her left eye ran like a tear to just above her cheek. That, along with bruises on her right shoulder which she absently stroked through the ripped seam of her shirt, were the only visible evidence of the violence she'd suffered.

Eyes closed, she listened for her poppa's voice as if he were there, guiding her through one of their stage acts. She had been his assistant for nearly four years now. In that short time, they had become one of the best colored touring acts in the Blackbelt, performing a variety of sleight-of-hand, escapes, and mind-reading tricks.

On stage, blindfolded, her back to the audience, Oureka would use her "psychic powers" to identify personal objects held by patrons. Standing in the audience, her father would encourage both she and the patron to concentrate on the object. Smiling inwardly, she would pause dramatically, fingers dancing near her temples just before accurately naming the object to the astonishment of the crowd. No one ever guessed that her poppa was communicating with her using a code that she had committed to memory All she had to do was listen.

I'm listenin', Poppa. I'm listenin'.

But there were no secret messages in the darkness behind her eyes, only the shrill memory of his voice rising above the shouts and sirens, her hand slipping out of his and—

Oureka opened her eyes, thankfully lost for a split second in the comforting blur between night and day. She did not want to look at the other passengers piled in the truck like brittle timber, leaning stiffly against one another for support, their ashen faces taut, each lost in an abyss of collective trauma. Some had tried to camouflage the suffering in clothes borrowed from those who had managed to pack a few precious belongings amidst the carnage that had engulfed them. Most were still garbed in the bloodied tatters of the summer dresses and skirts they had worn to work or market or wherever they may have been when the whirlwind of violence plucked them from the comfort of an ordinary day and into bedlam.

The truck sped across Eads Bridge towards the smoldering ruins of six thousand lives.

Below her dangling feet, the asphalt rushed by like a great white ocean. Oureka imagined herself and the others crushed in the bowels of a slave vessel crossing the Middle Passage. Poppa had told her of the countless imprisoned Africans who had hurled themselves into the sea rather than be ripped from their world.

Their uncounted spirits stretch like an eternal bridge between the past and future. The brilliance of their lives illuminates ours. Never forget.

I won't, Poppa. I won't.

And then Oureka was falling towards that eternal sea, falling away from the desolate now into the rushing asphalt/ocean below. She stopped short of oblivion, jarred from the waking dream.

She was hanging from the truck, torso almost parallel to the road below. The dainty woman in the gray dress gripped her arm tightly in her manicured hands. The woman's patient gaze had dissolved, given way to panic. She looked close to weeping as she hauled the girl back into the truck, folding her into a tight embrace. The life-death moment passed so quickly that only a handful of the other passengers had even witnessed it.

"Lord have mercy," someone testified. The National Guardsmen blew smoke rings into the blue sky over the Mississippi. The truck sped towards desolation.

"WON'T YOU TELL ME YOUR NAME, CHILD?" THE manicured woman asked a few hours later. They wandered through the ruins of downtown East St. Louis. Oureka said nothing, continued to scan the debris-strewn streets, empty stoops, and vacant doorways. She had held her tongue that way all through the long afternoon.

The truck had carried each of the refugees to what remained of their homes. They had watched survivors sift through the torched, looted wreckage of their lives, searching for discarded clothing, blankets, remnants of photographs, the remains of personal letters, small, priceless mementos. One after another, the refugees gathered what they could, piled sacks full of belongings into the truck before moving on to the next retrieval site.

The manicured woman had spoken quietly to each person, jotting brief notes in the pad that she carried in her satchel.

When Oureka had abandoned the truck at the end of their tour and set off on foot towards the heart of what had been the colored district, the woman had followed her.

"I'm Pearl Van Cleve," she said now as they moved through

the ruined downtown quarter self-consciously aware of the fact that they were perhaps the only colored people left in a city still simmering with race-hatred.

Face dimly lit with hope, the child gazed up at her companion with sudden interest. "You write for *Vanguard News*. Poppa sometimes reads your stories aloud to me."

"Where is your father, sweetheart?"

A dark veil fell over Oureka's face again. She backed away, shaking her head, searching either side of the street for an avenue of retreat. But there was no solace in the soot-black remains of torched storefronts and homes. She whirled, stumbling towards the corner of Broadway and Eighth Street, vanished behind some overturned wagons and automobiles.

When Pearl caught up to her a few minutes later, the girl was standing on the steps of the Divine Light Holiness Church on Sixth, peering into the gaping darkness beyond the ornate door which hung askew on a single twisted hinge.

"Poppa! Poppa!"

Each desperate outcry returned, a mocking echo.

Pearl Van Cleve stood by helplessly, watched the child's screams disintegrate into hoarse whispers and the whispers into barely audible moans. Oureka's proud shoulders collapsed. She crumpled slowly to the stoop.

Pearl kept her distance. She watched the child convulse with grief. After a while, Oureka pulled a folded slip of paper from her pocket and rocked slowly back and forth, clutching it to her chest.

Long minutes passed, the distant sounds of the living city— news vendors, hawking their wares from street corners; the

THE BRIDGE

rattle of trolley cars, the sputter of car engines cruising along busy avenues—intruded like surreptitious laughter at a funeral. Finally, Pearl Van Cleve cautiously approached. She kneeled on the steps beside the child and gently took the weathered handbill from the girl's limp grasp.

A well-dressed man, dark-skinned and rugged, stared back at her from the page. He was shackled, wrapped from head to foot in formidable chains. The girl standing beside the man in the photograph was the child who sat beside Pearl now. In the picture, Oureka's arms were akimbo, her head tilted slightly to one side. She looked upon the chained man with an expression of exaggerated skepticism. The text below the image read:

JOIN THE INCOMPARABLE NOBLE DARING AND
HIS FABULOUS DAUGHTER OUREKA FOR AN
EVENING OF MYSTERY AND MAGIC.

SUNDAY JULY 1

6 TO 8 PM

"Your father?" Pearl asked, placing a gentle hand on the girl's shoulder.

"He should be here," Oureka said as if the sun had disappeared in mid-afternoon. "Nothing ever held him for long. Not ropes, or chains, or iron crates. He always found a way out. He should be here."

Oureka studied her empty palm like a familiar story whose ending had suddenly changed. She felt her father's hand holding hers much too firmly and her eyes burned with the memory of racing through the thickening smoke that filled the church that night.

Come out niggers!
Come out or burn!

But more fire waited outside where the streets roared with the malevolent revelry of a Roman circus. Flames engulfed buildings on both sides of the street. Her father had scooped her into his arms without breaking stride. In his free hand, he held a length of pipe that he swung in wide, continuous arcs. Oureka remembered seeing one of the church matrons running naked through a gauntlet of violence. Her austere Sunday dress had been ripped from her body by the clawing hands of her pursuers, and what remained hung in ribbons from her waist. The woman's slender arms were bruised, bleeding from heavy stones that flew at her from every direction. Even after she fell to the ground, the flurry did not abate.

Oureka could still feel her father's heart pounding against her own while they ran past brutal tableaus of Old Testament horror.

"We were almost to the bridge," Oureka whispered. "Poppa put me down. Just to catch his wind. But there were so many people. Like animals stampeding. Crazy scared..." Her voice trailing off.

Pearl reached out, filling Oureka's empty hand with her own. They stood together.

"We were almost to the bridge," Oureka said, one last time.

And then they abandoned the stoop to search for shelter.

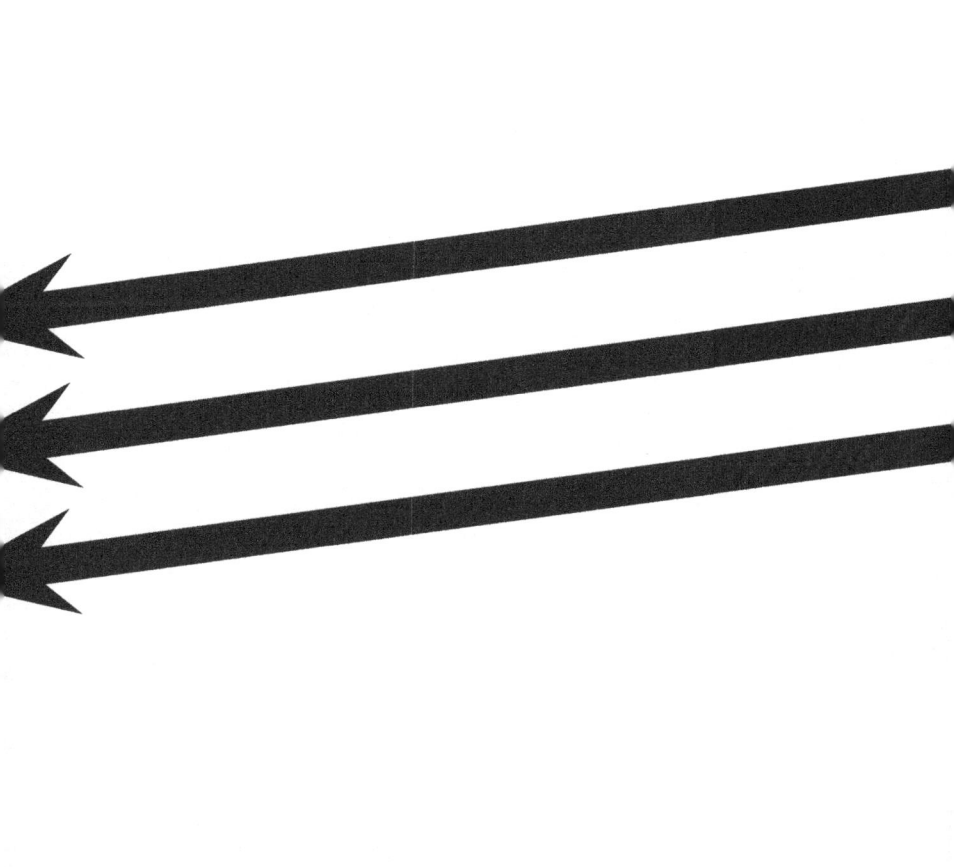

WEST OF NOGALES, AZ

by

Charles Duffie

WE DON'T CALL OURSELVES A CITIZEN MILITIA. WE carry rifles and Glocks, binoculars and pepper spray. But that's what you do in war. Listen. Something happened one night, and we woke up with our backs flat to the wall. Don't even know what it was. I suppose it wasn't just one thing, but it feels that way. Now here we are with nothing to do but hold the line. Maybe the last line. Stop those backpackers from coming across and taking what's left. I mean, Jesus, I lost my house in 2008 and four jobs since. My wife goes part-time at two diners and a daycare center. We can't afford a family. Thirty-six years old and I'm afraid to have a son. The American Dream of my father's generation? Come on. Maybe it was real. Once. But in this world, it makes a difference, having something that doesn't move. In this world, borders remind us of who we are. They give a shape to things. And these days, that's worth patrolling.

Jefferson said, "Let the eye of vigilance never be closed." Even if it's almost swollen shut.

It's a mile from the edge of town to the fence, a dirt and scrub no man's land. I drop Frank off. He'll walk the line looking for diggers while I drive recon along the service road. The fence is eighteen feet high, made of steel planks rusted almost red. There are six inches of space between each plank. Those gaps were a good idea. Makes it hard for anyone to hide. We turned seventeen illegals back last year. Two made it under. Our town doesn't have a border patrol office, so we dropped them at the police station. Sheriff Bell sent them to Nogales and bought us a couple of beers. The only thing he said about our scraped knuckles was those bad hombres had it coming.

The morning is heating up when Frank calls an S.O.S. on the walkie-talkie. It only takes a couple minutes to drive back. I cut across the scrub and dust right up to the fence. Frank is hunched over, hands pressed to his eyes. Through the gaps in the fence I see a tall man and a boy, skin brown as earth. Behind them, fifty yards out in the Mexican desert, a dozen more backpackers wait like scared rabbits, clutching their sad bundles.

I pull my Glock as I climb out of the truck. I'm ready to go. "What's going on?"

Frank straightens up. His eyes are red and swollen. "I was walking the fence," he says. "Goddamnit, this stings!" He pours water on a black bandana that's already wet. "I come across some diggers." He presses the dripping cloth against his eyes. "I throw a rock to scare them off. Someone throws one back. Hits me in the chest. They all start running except this smiling jackrabbit."

He nods to the tall man on the other side. The man has one hand on the boy's shoulder. "I figure he threw the rock," Frank says. "So I pull a can of pepper spray. But the spray comes back through the fence into my own goddamn eyes."

The breeze burns the shirt on my back. "Not sure what you're saying here, Frank."

"Watch," he says, and pushes me away like whatever he's going to show me could blow up in our faces. He picks up a rock. "I won't go any closer to that damn fence."

He's pretty close already, about three feet. He tosses the rock underhand, aiming for the gap between two metal planks. As soon as the rock hits that open space, it comes back. No ping, no thunk, like it bounced off thin air. Frank catches it and looks at me.

"Jesus Christ," I say. It must be the light, I don't know. "Do that again."

Frank backs up and fires the rock overhand. It dings on the fence and ricochets into the dirt. "Goddamnit," he says and throws another rock. It hits the gap between two planks and comes back, not like it's bouncing off something but like someone on the other side threw a line drive just as hard. Frank ducks but the rock nicks his bare shoulder. Blood beads up.

"That's impossible," I say. My mind feels like a box ripped open but there's nothing inside. That rock hit thin air and came back just as hard.

The tall man on the other side of the fence just smiles. Maybe he thinks it's a miracle. Maybe that's why he and his boy are still here.

Frank touches the red on his shoulder. He holds the pads of

his big fingers close to his face like he's never seen blood before. I've known Frank since grade school. He used to be in construction. After his divorce, he lived with Beth and me for six months. When I lost another shit job last year, he gave us the bedroom in his apartment until we got back on our feet. It was when we were out of work, with all that empty time on our hands, that Frank started our weekend patrol. "You got to keep busy," he'd always say, calm and steady. "Keep turning the pages. Keep the story moving or you'll go crazy." But there's a wildness in his swollen eyes now, like all the pages are coming loose.

I have to do something. Prove something. I step up to the fence, tap a rusty panel the way you tap a pan to see if it's hot, then press my palm against the metal. It's warm in the sun, solid as the ground under my feet. I look at Frank. He nods his chin. I slide my hand toward the six-inch space between two panels. As my fingers pass through, they vanish and come back the other way, right above my knuckles. It looks like my fingers have been chopped off and pushed back at me. But there's no blood. No cuts. No pain. It's like a magic trick, something done with mirrors. I actually smile. Then I flex my hand and my fingertips tap my knuckles.

I snap my hand back. I'm not smiling anymore.

Frank throws the wet cloth in the dirt. Pulls a hunting knife from his bandolier. On the other side of the fence, the tall man and boy step back but the man keeps smiling.

"Look at him," Frank says. "He thinks it's funny."

Frank takes a couple of breaths like he's about to go off a high dive and steps closer to the fence. He eases the blade into the gap. The end of the knife vanishes and comes back the other way, right on top of itself. He stares at it, puffy eyes twitching. Then he keeps moving the blade forward, which simultaneously moves its razor edge back toward his hand.

"Frank," I say.

He keeps going until the tip slices into the knuckle of his thumb. The flesh opens like taut meat. I think I see the white of tendon or bone, but Frank's nod pulls my eyes to his face. I don't like what I see.

He draws the knife back and glares at it as if the steel had betrayed him.

On the other side, the jackrabbit steps around his boy and approaches the fence. His smile is different now and I know he's scared too. He and Frank stare at each other through a six-inch gap, faces shiny with sweat. The man reaches straight out and pushes his hand through the narrow space up to the wrist. It disappears and comes back toward him like he's reaching for his own shoulder. He stares at it and something in his smile cracks. His jaw tightens hard to hold what's left of that grin in place. He lifts his eyes to Frank and waits.

"Goddamnit," Frank mutters. He drops the knife in the dirt and reaches through a gap past his wrist. His hand comes back the other way. Blood drips from his thumb knuckle onto his forearm. In the desert quiet, the drip keeps awful time, pat-pat, pat-pat.

They both step toe-to-toe with the fence and slowly push until their arms look cut off at the elbows. Right above the stumps the forearms and hands emerge out of thin air, groping back at themselves. The man's palm presses against his own chest. Frank's fist clutches his own shirt. Some kind of short circuit is shutting down my brain. The gun falls like a stone from my hand.

Frank stumbles back as if the man had shoved him. The man withdraws his hand and cradles it like it's broken. His boy runs up and drags his away.

"Jesus Christ," I say again, and this time I'm not cursing. "Come on, Frank. Let's go."

But Frank is looking all around like invisible bees are swarming. "How big do you think it is?" he says.

"What? Frank, let's go!"

"How wide, goddamnit?!"

He doesn't wait for an answer. He steps closer, picks up the knife, and inserts the blade just enough to see it come back the other way. He moves left to the next gap and repeats his test. On the ninth gap, the blade doesn't come back. It behaves the way it's supposed to behave. He jabs his hand through several times, fast, like he's stabbing something to death on the other side.

"There," he growls. "There, goddamnit." He hacks a silver X in the rusted panel, then keeps going a few more spaces, pushing the knife at the gaps. The blade keeps going through.

Satisfied, he returns to the X, then works his way back along the fence, jabbing the air, watching the tip of the blade come back. I'm counting in my head. He stabs twenty gaps until the blade goes through again.

"There," he says and saws another X in the rusted panel. He waves the knife at the ten-foot space between the two Xs, like he's just corralled a dangerous animal. "There! That's as far as it goes."

"All right," I say. "All right, Frank. Put the knife away and let's—"

"Wait," he says, but not to me. He drops the knife in the dirt. "Wait one goddamn second." He grabs a rock, notes the space between the Xs, and pitches the rock hard as he can, high in the air. When it crosses above the fence, it comes back the other way, moving along the same upward arc but over *our* heads now, like its trajectory has been reversed. We watch it fall and bounce behind us in the scrub.

"How far up do you think it goes?" Frank says. "How far down?" His red eyes are buzzing in his head. He glares over my shoulder. "Goddamnit. That jackrabbit's still smiling."

I wouldn't call it a smile.

As Frank walks past, I grab his arm. He shoves by me, moves to the fence, and nods his chin at the tall man.

"English?"

The man's broken smile widens on one side. "Some."

"You know what's happening here?"

"No."

"No. You ever see anything like this?"

"No."

"No. You know why? Because no one has. You know why? Because it's goddamn impossible. But you think that's funny, don't you?"

The man sort of laughs but stops like he lost his voice. Frank has drawn a pistol from his side holster. He points at a gap between two planks. Level with his waist. Right at the boy's head.

I step forward. "Frank!" He flinches. Jesus, shouting at a man with a gun. I feel the width of the boy's eyes in my own.

"This isn't right," Frank says. "Maybe we can break through." I don't think he even sees the kid. He's staring at that gap. "Maybe it's up to us. To put things right."

"Frank." I cup my hand over his wrist. "I don't know what's going on. I'm losing my mind here. But if you pull that trigger, one of two things will happen. The bullet will bounce off the air and you'll shoot yourself. Or. Frank, listen to me. Or the bullet will go through and you'll kill that kid."

"How do you know?" he says. He looks at me and it's like I can see right into the flooded basement of his heart and the water is rising fast. "How do you know anything anymore?"

Our faces are so close I see the pores in his skin. The peppered pouches around his eyes are taut and wet like they're going to burst. I can't hold his red gaze, so I stare at his lips and ease the gun down. The pulse in his wrist beats against my fingers. Down, down.

His lips flatline and the gun fires.

The bullet comes back at the same angle but on our side of the fence, blasting Frank's knee. The man and boy run. Frank's in the dirt, clutched up on his side, punching the gun at the fence, BAM BAM BAM BAM BAM. Bullets spark on the rusted panels, bounce off the open gaps, whine like tiny sirens past my ears. I drop flat, tasting dust. BAM BAM BAM BAM.

Frank's hand click-click-clicks, and I hear him growling now. Even after I pry the pistol from his grip, he keeps flexing his hand, like he's firing invisible bullets at something he can't see. I cinch my belt around his thigh. His jaw bulges so tight his teeth snap. Beyond the fence, there's no sign of the backpackers. We drive to town. Frank keeps pressing the wound, his face blanching with pain. "There," he says. "There...there... there..."

I slap his hand away. "Leave it alone!"

After a few seconds, he starts up again. "There..."

Across that mile of scrub, the gunshots would have sounded like firecrackers. I call Sheriff Bell anyway, tell him we had a stupid accident and I'm taking Frank to the hospital. Bell says something about dropping by later to fill out a report.

At the hospital, Frank says he was messing around, trying to do a quick draw. They remove the bullet, but the knee is in bad shape. They give Frank a bed until a specialist can determine if surgery is needed. Frank tells them what they already know: he has no insurance. They say they're not making any promises.

When the room clears out, I come in and take a seat. Through the window I see the distant line of that border fence and yank the curtains. We just sit there. It's not like the movies. We don't search "quantum mysteries" on our phones. We don't buy coffee from the vending machine and argue about the meaning of life. We don't talk about going back with a camera and making a YouTube video. When you find a crack in the universe in real life? You back the fuck up.

Frank closes his eyes. He's loaded with meds, so I think he's sleeping. But into the quiet he says, "I'm leaving. Going north."

I take that in. "Where?"

He opens his eyes halfway and grins, and for a moment he looks like his old self. "I don't know," he says. "Alaska, maybe?"

After the surgery, Frank walks with a limp. A week later, my best friend is gone.

I get a job at the new Amazon distribution warehouse on the edge of town. It's long hours and low pay and shit conditions, but I need the work. Six days a week I eat a sack lunch outside, watching the fence across a mile of desert like I'm afraid it's going to move. Friends ask what I'm staring at all the time and I say nothing. I slot down into routines and habits, scrambling full-time for part-time pay. I don't even tell Beth.

Some nights I can't sleep. I listen to my wife breathe and stare up into the dark until the ceiling looks like the sky. It gets to where I'm so awake I can't stand it. I walk an hour into the scrub and sit between those fading Xs, bouncing pebbles off the air. I've lost all faith in the shape of things and I don't know how to move on from that.

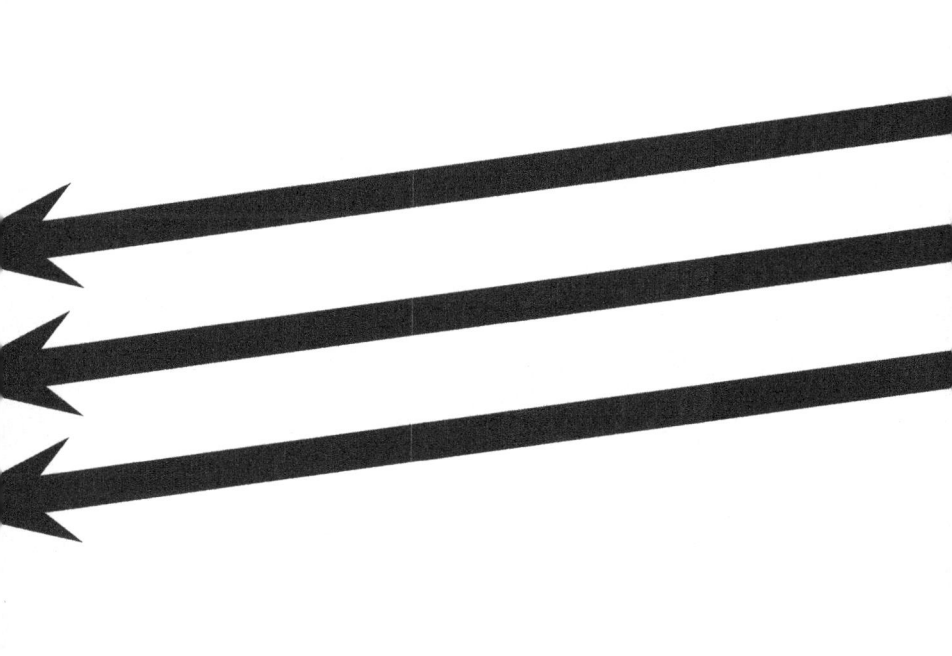

GOOD COP

by

Jeff Ewing

THE SHOULDER-TO-SHOULDER FELT GOOD AFTER SO long listening to the sounds of his own movements, his thoughts the only ones getting any time.

The line rippled, an animal twitching with something like hunger. Earlier in the day Kendall had put on the Discovery Channel in the station and they'd watched cheetahs chase down springboks, crocodiles snatch pelicans off the water, nature doing what it did best. The crowd was beautiful, the waiting was beautiful, anticipating, knowing...

"Kneel with us, kneel with us!"

A few cheered as the line dropped in unison to a knee, pulled on their masks. His own fogged with laughter in front of him, batons tapped the pavement in cadence.

In the winter, fog would roll over town and muffle the racket, his footsteps, the voice in his head. He remembered one morning a deer darting out of the brush along the river, its wide terrorized eyes. The fog condensed on his bare arms. His eyes burned and his heart thudded inside its hollow, awakened cage.

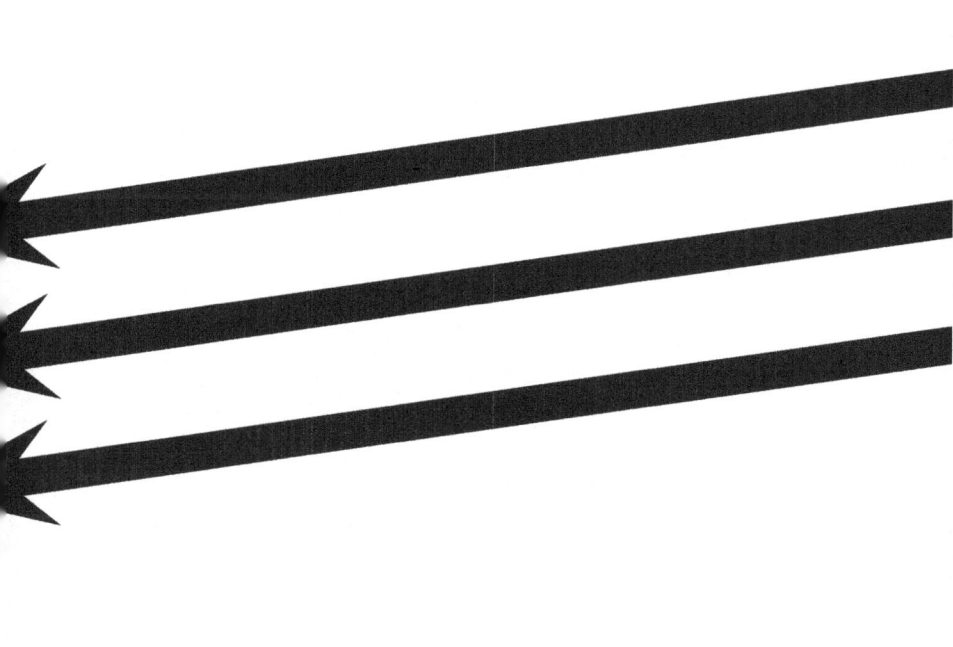

POETRY

THE ONE WHERE THE ROUGHNECKS BURN THE WORLD TO THE GROUND WHILE LOOKING FAB AS FUCK

by

Kanyinsola Olorunnisola

I got ark, I got evil, that rot inside my DNA
  –Kendrick Lamar

everyone's hip these days everyone's lit these days this counterculture thing is getting colonized all over again who are the bad guys this time too many people on this side of the divide want me dead i taste too much like the enemy here comes the bloodless genocide perfumed rage kiss stained cigarettes glittered glock gucci masks mug shots pose click work guerillas looking fab as fuck talking war strategy over samosas & grape-soaked punch lakunle & badiru televise the revolution from their iphones bomb filters for the explosion fireworks scattered all over the street we lost our gangster poets in the crossfire no language left to romanticize trauma to make art of the labyrinth of our lives which do we bite the bullet or the dust we are bringing the war to you we are bringing you pain we are bringing you ruin we are woman we are black we are heathen we are faithless we are femme we are masc we are other we are center we are

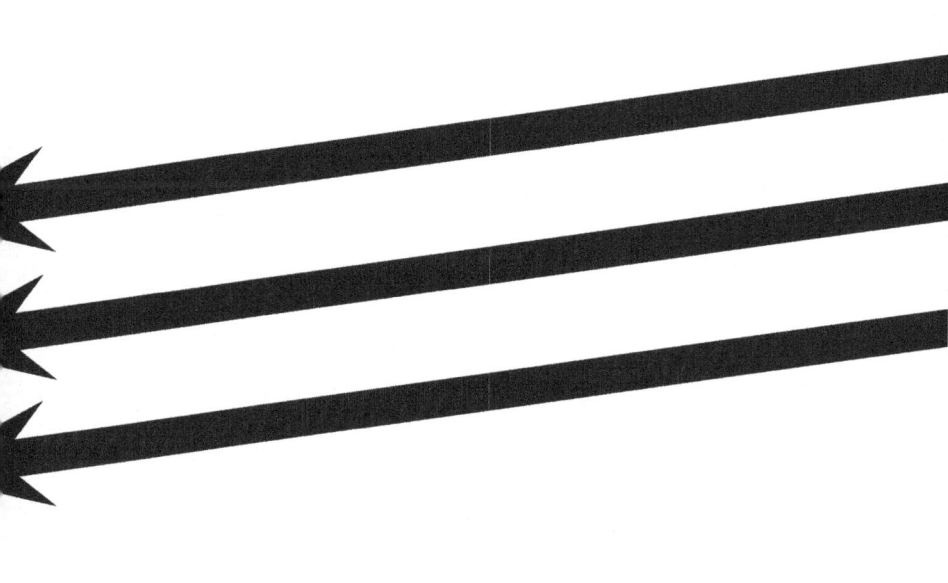

COFFIN AT DUSK
by
Jonathan Endurance

After Ahmaud Arbery

After the war, I drag my father out
of the sand, the cloud of dust cataloguing

his face like a museum of ancient relics.
Because every war pulls our feet

a step closer to God, I kneel by his side
and imagine his mouth a music box

void of melodies. I whisper into
his ears. His silence poisons my thought.

What is silence if not the blood streaming
through his mouth. And the bullet holes

in his chest like doors ushering him into a new
beginning. I desire to unlearn every hymn that

busies my mouth with requiems. Because the
face of death could be anyone's father,

I wipe the dust off his face. I recite the Lord's Prayer
with a mouth full of gasoline and matchstick.

FILL IN THE BLANKS

by

James Redfern

Meanwhile, on [date and time],
another brother was murdered.

Four [or more (adjust number)] members
of a white power hate group,
[insert name law enforcement agency]
murdered another brother.

The news anchor said the DA said:
"[the truth is inadmissible]."

Soundbite: "[insert name of murdered brother]
resisted / posed a threat / was on PCP /
had what looked to be a gun / other
(circle one or more)."
Headline reads: "[blame victim]."

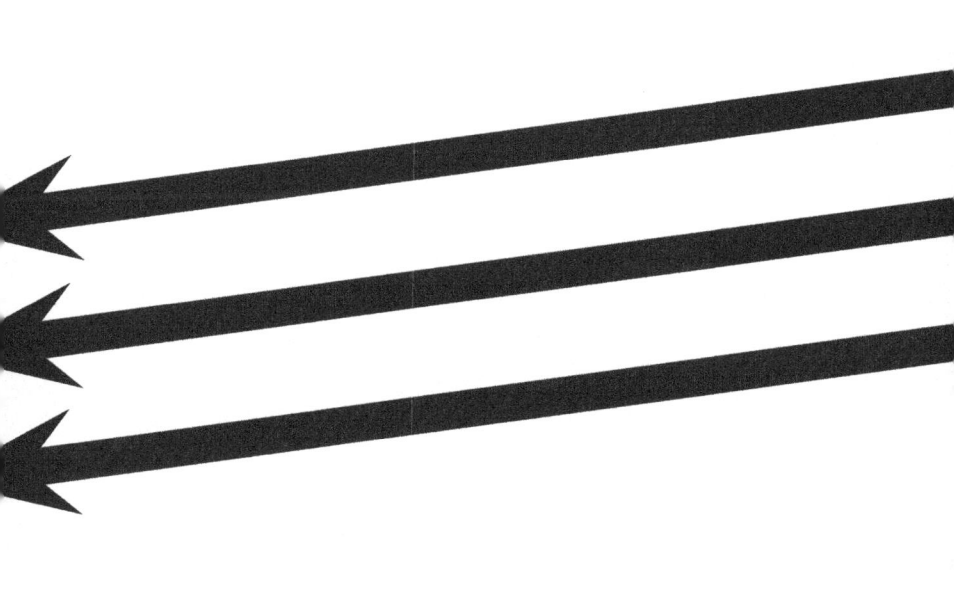

DISCRIMINATING

by

Larry Smith

Weeding around the bird feeder,
some fresh green with pebbled buds,
yet I dig my fingertips down
in dark earth and yank them out,
separating good from bad like a
camp guard or an executioner.

Do I think too much, or am I
just awakening to our human control,
and the power of my whiteness?

And at the feeder, do I see
only birds of brightest color,
telling my grandson, "Oh those
are common starlings and wrens;
watch for cardinals and orioles."

WE ARE ANTIFA

Am I the fish unaware of water,
the child blind at birth,
the vulture circling the dead?
These weedings weigh on me so,
and I melt in this noonday sun.

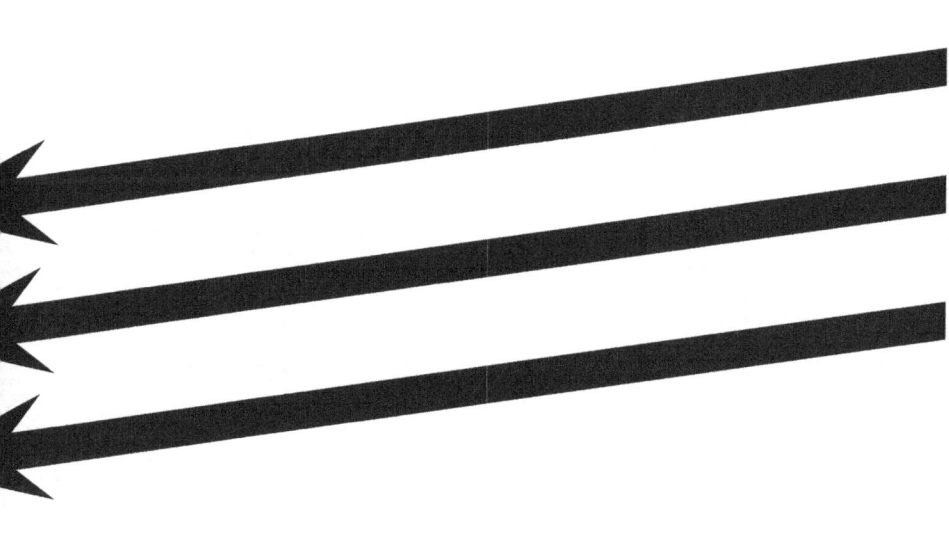

VILLAIN VILLANELLE

by

Edward Moreta Jr.

After Madvillainy

all this villainy / ain't no kidding me
coming down the street / (walking epiphany).
blood dj spin / swim in we. / rocking black seas

is our history. / we stray debris /
ain't no liberty / they stole us from / our vicinity.
all this villainy / ain't no kidding… / me?

can't get a degree / can't live / carefree /
without their saying / i got no dignity. /
blood dj spin / hymn on beat / dying black sea

not hyperbole. / in every city / in pine trees /
on the news / dead soliloquies.

WE ARE ANTIFA

all this villainy / are you shitting me?!

federal legacy / built / on felony
and you think i kill my brothers / more than supremacy?
blood money spin / lock n key / drowning black sea

is what they want to see. / but they nobody
they fry wit da heat! all this white noise / don't let us sleep.

all this villainy / is killing we.
but blood dj spin / black jubilee / we ain't the wreck / we the bouying.

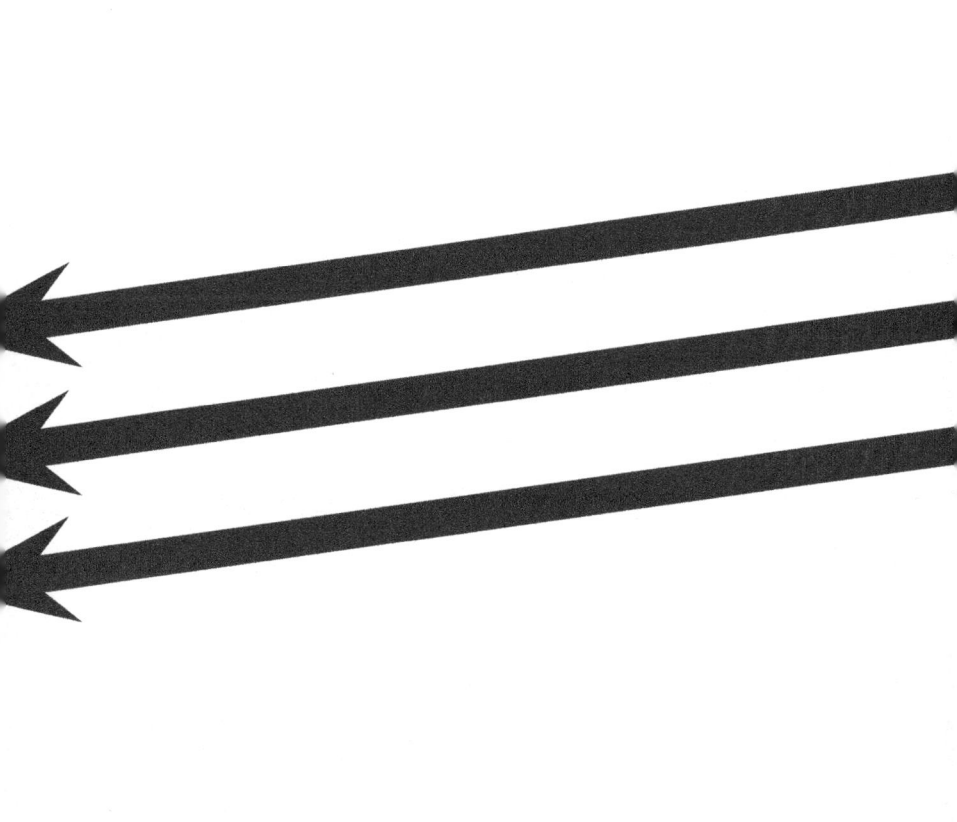

THE PEACE SCULPTURE WORE: OCTOBER, 1996

by

Andrés Castro

In the end the last birds
will be mocking birds.
  —R.B.

June 11, 1963.
On a busy South Vietnamese
street, a Buddhist monk
sat like charcoal in flames
smoke, palms together in
protest of religious persecution,
as bystanders watched.

Did you know his myth—Kathleen?
How his heart found whole
was placed in a shrine?
How The New York Times *would*

run your story? Soon enough
find you more or less insane?

Local reports cite
anonymous police sources saying…
evidence was found
that Ms. Kathleen Chang
experimented with cuts
of meat and flammable
liquids—for the past year.

It was the picture of you
in a bathing suit
that first stopped me.

Fifteen years of waving protest flags,
of dancing stars & stripes bikini,
of yelling social transformation
manifesto on the grounds of Penn U.
She became a fixture there some said,
not attracting the crowds she once did.

Your sad eyes seemed to watch me
as I read—you danced as I read
strutted and kicked—perhaps calling
me sexist, perhaps not.

Why October 22nd of '96?
Why Tuesday? Why choose
11:20 a.m. to walk across campus,

THE PEACE SCULPTURE WORE: OCTOBER, 1996

stand before sculptured peace
sign between two trees, pour
bucket of gasoline over your slim
build, and set yourself aflame?

...Ms. Kathleen Chang
experimented with cuts of meat
and flammable liquids.

In a letter she gave out
to local media and friends:
This is the tactically
correct move. I feel it with all
the weight of my soul.

Fifty witnesses watched,
as a university policeman tried
to smother the flames with his jacket,
but the flames started up again.

Sweet Kathleen, some said
you tried to dance.

By late afternoon
as light rain fell,
the peace sculpture wore
more than a dozen bouquets,
strands of beads,
and a poem that began:
Maybe she was crazy,

the girl said,
but I don't think so.

The last birds are
here, Kathleen.
The last birds
are here.

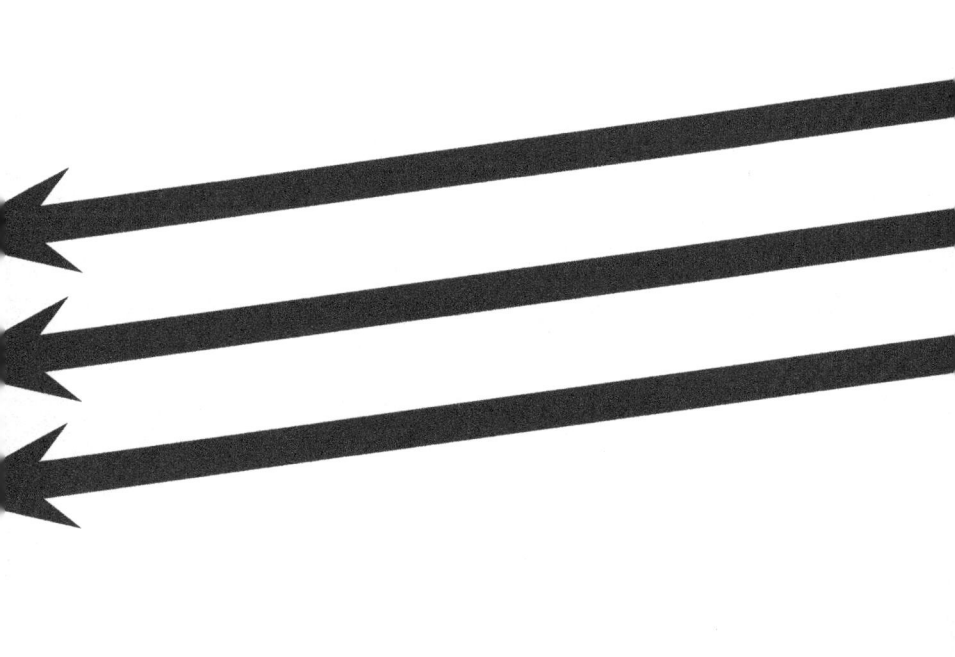

AT NIGHTFALL

by

Thea Matthews

armies of cops in riot gear   stand ready to block
us   from gathering in the street.

who is protecting who   when no one is safe
in the face of a baton   and a Glock 22?

each bullet has a name   a face at the point
the marches prevail   regardless   of weak joints.

herds of uniforms barricade the pathways
yet we find another way   always

to rise   solidarity the weapon   the subversive stride
expose backdoor deals of the POA   no one can hide.

rebels resist   they are determined to kill

who is trying to kill   our city   first.

who's city   our city.
who's streets   our streets.

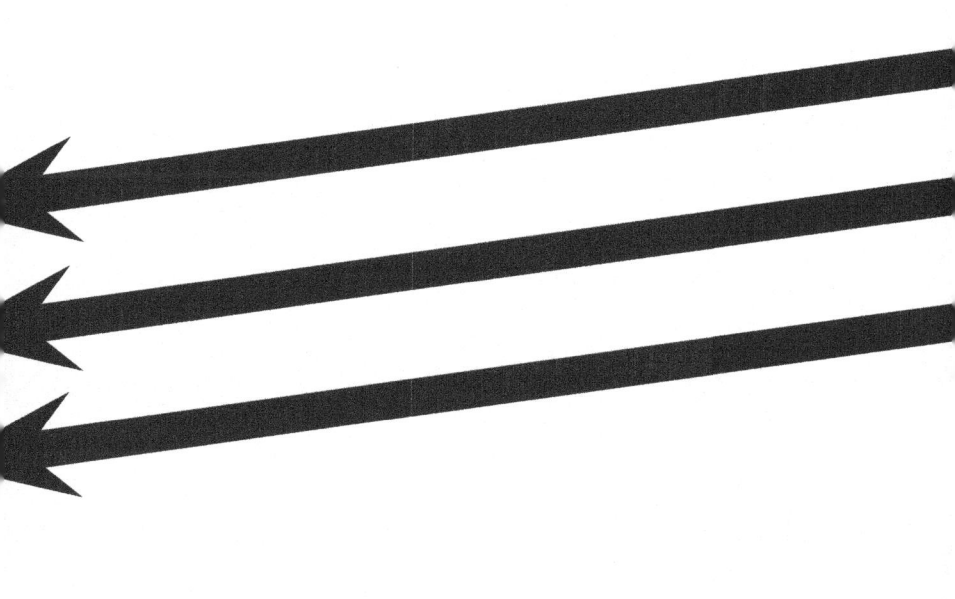

A PRESIDENT LIKE NO OTHER

by

Alan Meyrowitz

Each lie became a brick

this one placed atop another,
that one to the side

until, indeed, three years in
he had his wall

What had seemed an edifice
so many deemed benign,
an artifice of politics
a realist might expect

must now be seen as emblem
of democracy's decline,
mortared with our own neglect

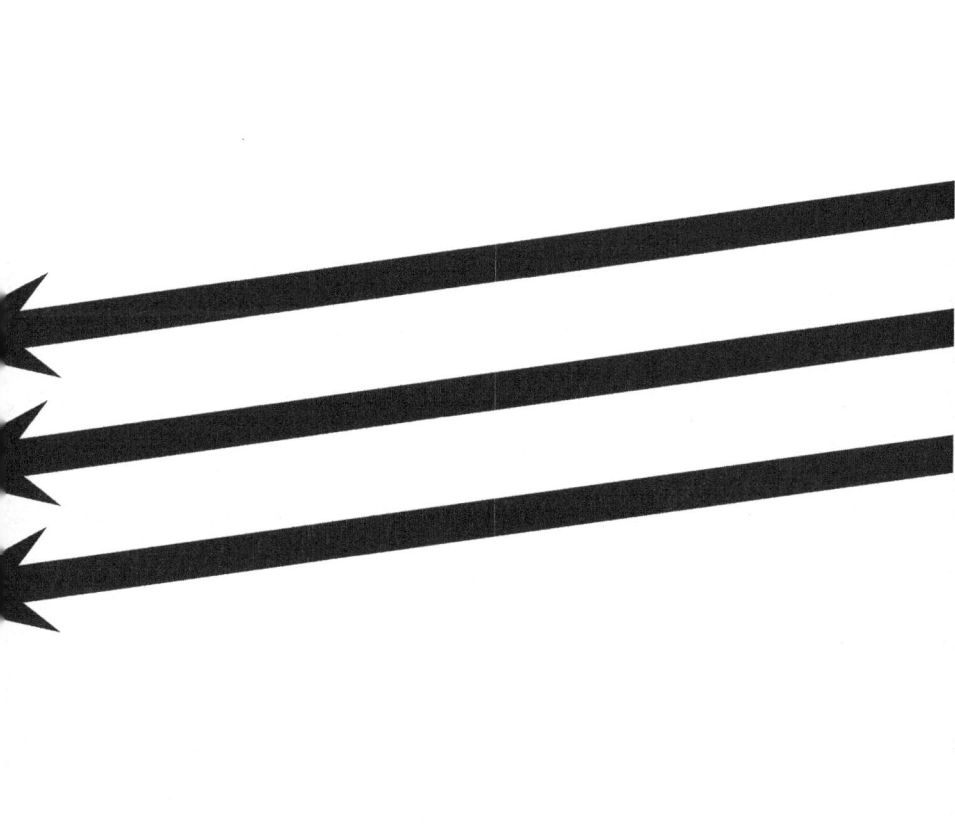

LEAD AND TESTICLES

by

Ramon Jimenez

The Border Patrol man
holds so much power.
In charge of protecting us
yet poorly trained and educated,
ill-equipped for a world full of change
while given a loaded gun that readies to kill.

Does this make him a hero?
The main star in some action movie from the '80s
where he gets to play some tough guy
that guards that scribbled line with lead and testicles.

And what makes him so big and tough?
So tough that he dumps tear gas on kids
shoots people for throwing rocks
bashes the heads of dehydrated souls

while he separates children by force
sends them off to makeshift concentration camps.

And if you ask him
he is here to protect his country
yet why was he caught on the cartel pay roll
habitually neglectful
to shipments of black tar and bricks of coke?

And isn't his surname Spanish?
Lopez, Rodriguez, Hernandez, Jimenez?
It must be easy for him
to detain friends, cousins, brothers.
Can he even hang out in the barrio?
Or do they call him pocho, malinche, sicario?

A version of this poem was first published in The Anti-Languorous Project, *Issue #5:* Pithy Politics, *October, 2020.*

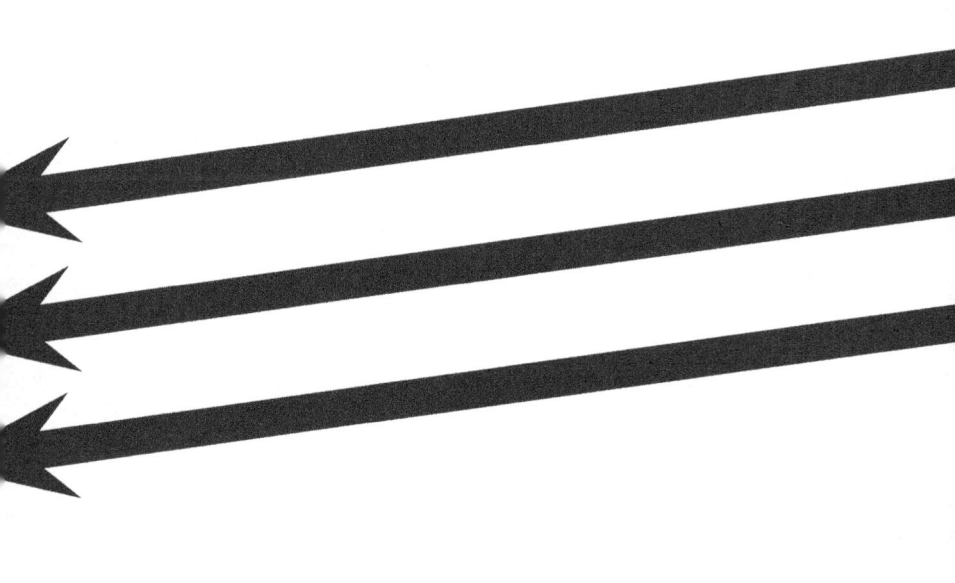

I CAN'T BREATHE: ATTICA PEACE TREATY

by

Jonathan Andrew Pérez, Esq.

The 1973 Attica Uprising was one of the most significant in the prisoner's rights movement of the 1970s. In total there were four days of negotiations. 1,281 of the Attica Prison's 2,200 inmates rioted, taking 42 hostage, following the killing of George Jackson. Finally, police took over.

We are men! We are not beasts.[1]   A treaty with
   the waning jaundiced moon.
In the golden age of Grand Juries, fabricated evidence
     this was no living condition, this was nothing but an idea un-chained.

At night, tincups clang.   Atop scores of salt-cloaked sweated
bedsheets on the windows, SOS, SEND HELP,   a retaking of speech,

---

[1] Elliott James Barkley, 1971, the 21-year-old orator and voice of the inmates during the Attica Uprising. After the inmates were surrounded, an eyewitness saw Barkley shot dead.

WE ARE ANTIFA

We are men! We are not beasts.

Among the scores
of broken signals, there was an inheritance
a grandfathered-in reality
      busted among the gas-negotiated air.

That the totality of the circumstances had before it
      a sign of life among the debris:

your father's father sent a letter — an Order, a *Habeus Corpus*.

Born on the day you were lost in the battlements,
      your name hidden under metal tables.

This un-drafting of the social contract.
This pretextual stop on the way to the medical treatment ward,

the invention of the force came not from physics, but a moneyed science.

One that patrolled Boston Harbor,
      that taxed the working poor,

      and manifested a motto, to protect and serve,
sold snake oil to the Taverns, sold snake oil in the form of liberty and safety
      caped crusading the moneyed riches of shipping interests.

In the end, what tide must rise to end the hostile undertow

      what hostage situations' chaotic peaks will break the underclass of men.

I CAN'T BREATHE: ATTICA PEACE TREATY

Our last showing became unmoored: *We are men! We are not beasts.*

And in the full warmth of humanity's moonlight, we scream, where everyone can come and see.

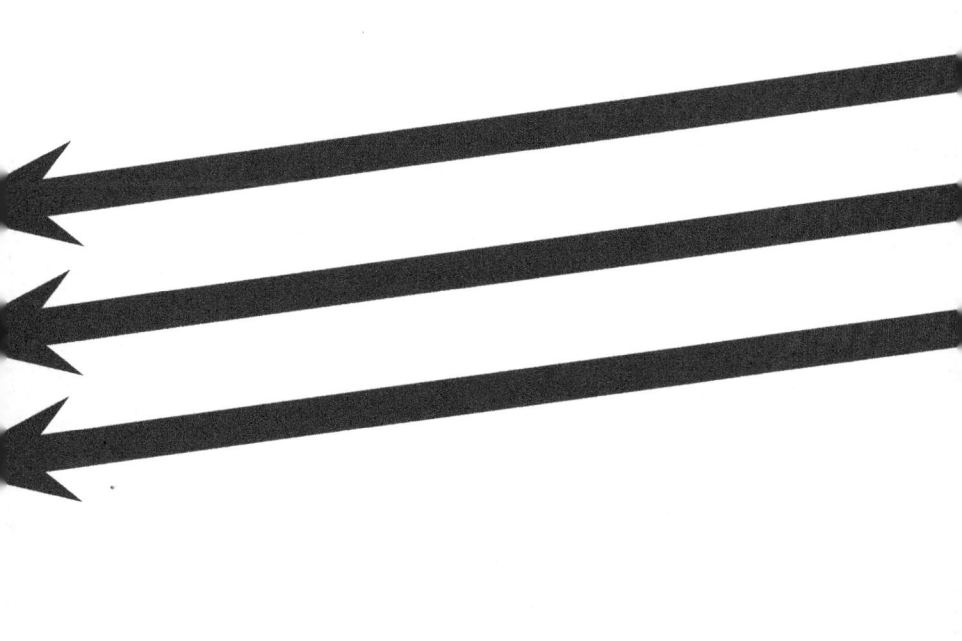

BRUTALITY
by
Geoffrey Aitken

the police
are busy
dispersing
angry
riotous
righteous
crowds
on streets
in public places
directed
instructed
by lawmakers
who
legitimise
Big Pharma
Arms Traders

Big Tobacco
Corporate Control

those law enforcement officers
are
after
the wrong people

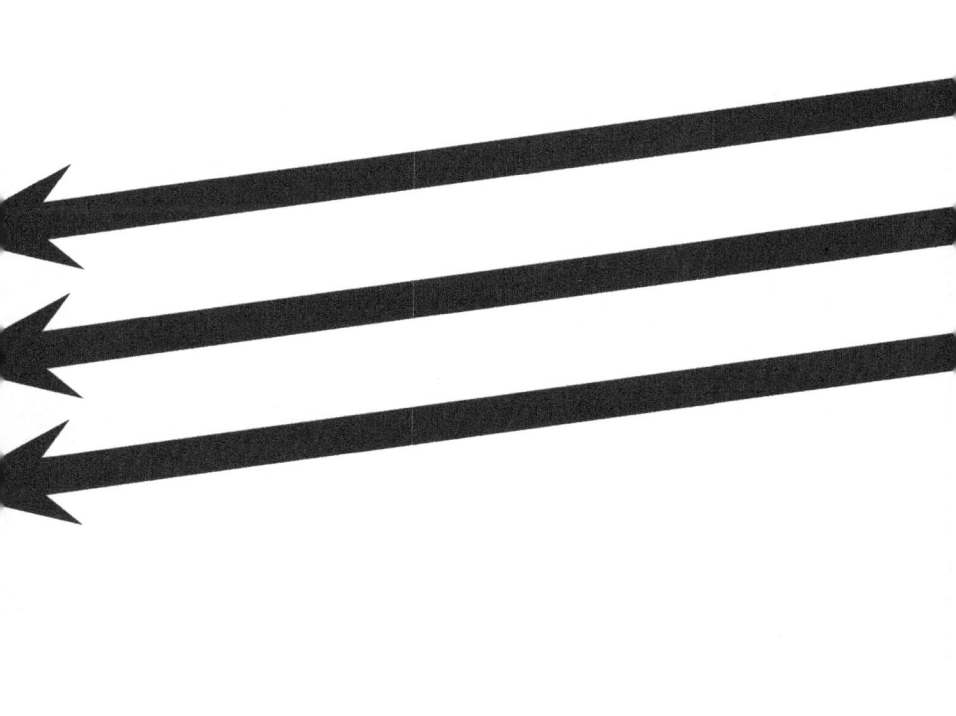

ABRACADABRA

by

Renoir Gaither

Precisely at the point when you begin to develop a conscience, you must find yourself at war with your society.
   —James Baldwin

Today is called *The Suffering Rhinoceros*. Heaps of twisted metal gleam on Lake St. Stolen land. A pile of bricks, charred, sun-swollen, speechless. Ashes convalesce on tiles from before YouTube. Tell the police. Those were pearls that were his eyes. Near the convenience store. Yessiree, a virus reified is one of Mapplethorpe's Polaroids. Old folks cling to binary thinking; *A man ain't a woman, a honeycomb ain't a jail.* Youth chant, their dreams an eleemosynary black art. Art annihilates every quid pro quo except its own. Say his name. George Floyd. Say. His. Name. Fuck 12. Abolish the police. Reclaim who you are—Decolonize. Punch a Nazi. Can you Hear us Now? ACAB tagged beneath a pink umbrella. Free the Looters. Reparations Now.

Reform Died. Abracadabra. Who shall read *Salvage the Bones?* All lives don't matter until Black Lives Matter. From a burning pawn shop the children run. 3rd Precinct gone dark. A Proud Boy shoots another in Seattle near the No Cop Co-op where a crow sentinels on a rooftop. *They're going to come and gentrify the whole place, buy up everything for nothing.* Someone left a rose on Jimi's statue. Near the autonomous zone. Mighty-O Donuts. The whole world's watching, y'all. Tomorrow will be called *Know Justice, Know Peace.*

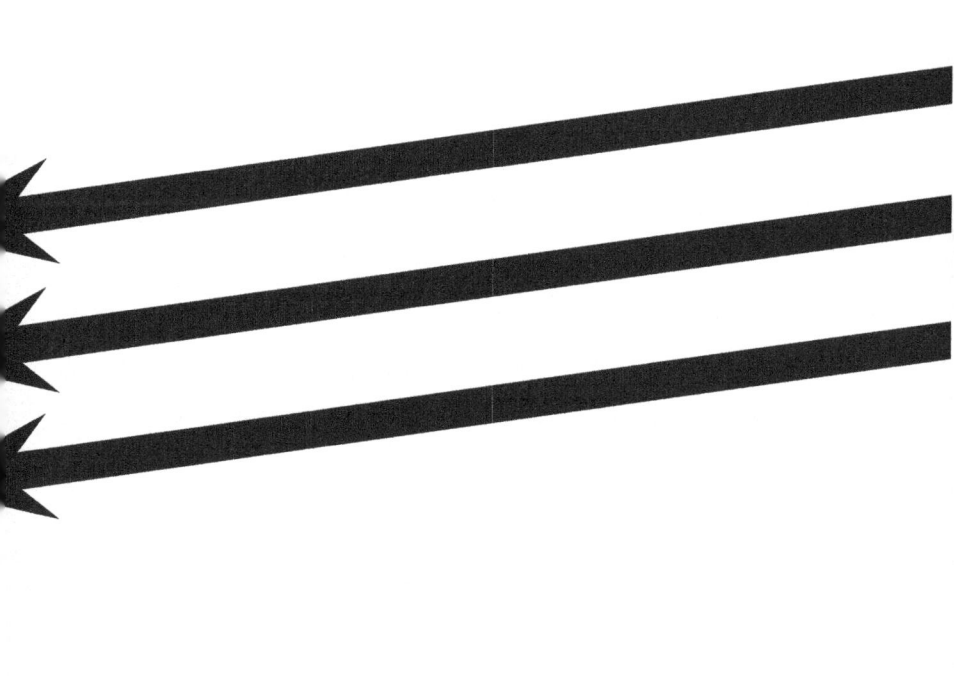

THIS RAGE IS A NECESSARY MONSTER

by

Connor Drexler

Daybreak descends a fog, rounding corners
and dulling edges, a scene one could call
beautiful. The morning after we heard
of poll lines in Milwaukee four hours
in length with thick, wet sleet, so I'd rather
call this wet cloud inconvenient. I'd rather
remember the fingers the cruel world
chopped away, counting only empty stumps
where the forest had once stood. Because
this rage is a necessary monster,
our blood coming as far as this
with an occasional one hell of a fight.
The momentary soft animal within
fangs lit like sunlight painful to behold,
ready to bite. Defiance is the blade
that doesn't slaughter, the final iron

hope never wished to hammer, revealed
now because death claims every hero
we'll ever have sooner than the wicked.
Because mercy must survive this, carried
that evening as the weight of venerable
bodies, as the patience that arrives
after panic falls on its own sharp ends.
I'm certain *because* my soul is weary.
Because I've found salvation in the pause
after my heart has shattered. Absolute
with each shadow we cast, bending light
no differently than any god. We too
so terribly this redeemable world.

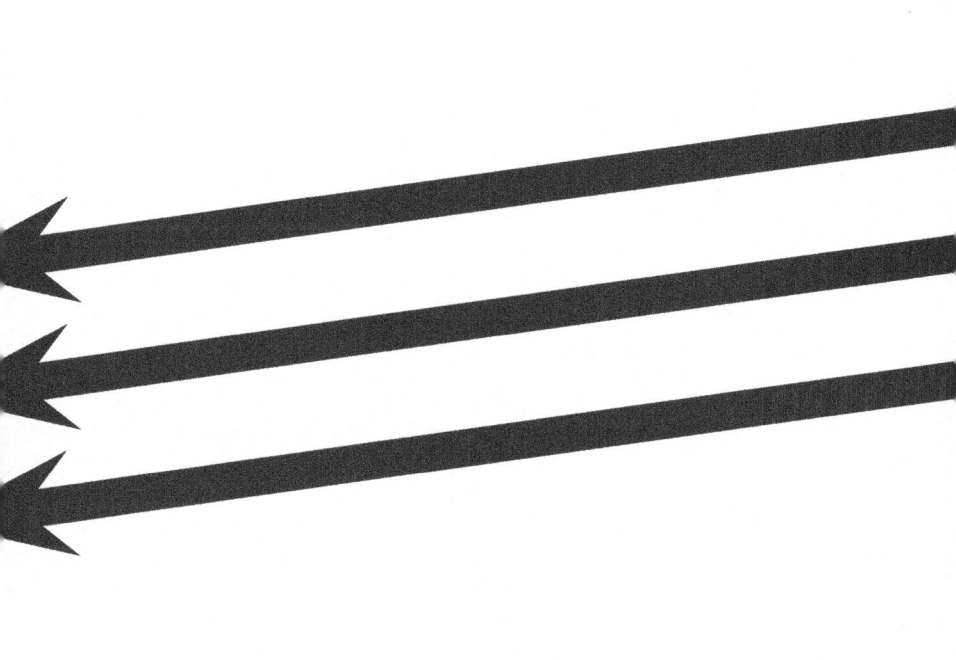

MAGNOLIA STATE

by

Gary Bloom

They say only the rich can afford magnolia trees
not because of how much the trees cost
but to pay someone to pick up the perpetually
falling leaves.

In Mississippi there are the finest antebellum mansions
built with cotton money
a nice way of saying
slave money.

Out back the cramped slave quarters
are an unwelcome reminder.

The lawns are full of magnolia trees
and those who pick up the leaves
in the unforgiving sun.

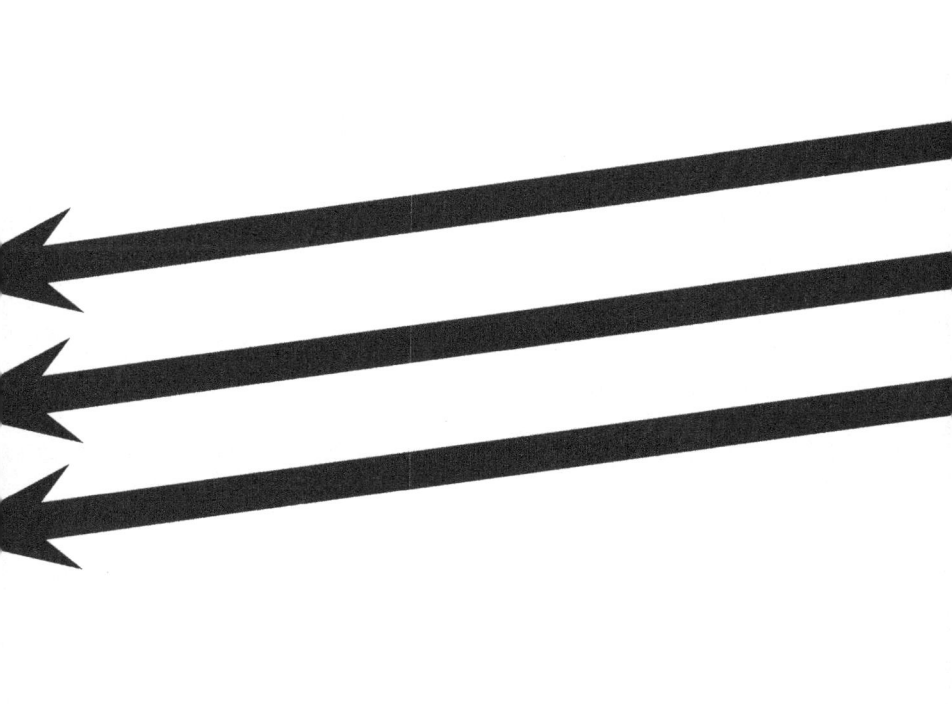

# ITEMIZING MY IDENTITY

by

Rhea Dhanbhoora

There are many things I cannot currently do:

Write well enough to sufficiently express outrage, for / against a country I call home now sinking under the heavy weight of fascism they will tell you does not exist; worry about my diaspora in despair you do not know is quickly dying / dead; say it is unfair when family members die living to a ripe old over-80 because how dare I / I have been lucky; travel because we are pandemic stuffed / I am an alien lacking the luxury of re-entry.

There are things I have done once that I will never do again:

Climb mountains, reach the top shelf of the pantry, stand several hours, breathe, walk, sleep without stenosis slowly surging up and down my one-disc-shy spine; sit at the same table as grandfather, grandmother, great-uncles, certain friends passed on to places I don't believe exist; drive a small yellow car no longer mine.

There are things I try not to do:

Succumb to anxiety attacks; take the things I have / have had for granted; be impatient, unkind; talk too much / too little of life in diaspora; spend sleepless nights wondering what if / how come / if only.

There are things
I have not; will not; can no longer even try.
There are things
still here, once around, never seen, now gone,
always part of me.

This poem was first published in Capsule Stories, *autumn 2020.*

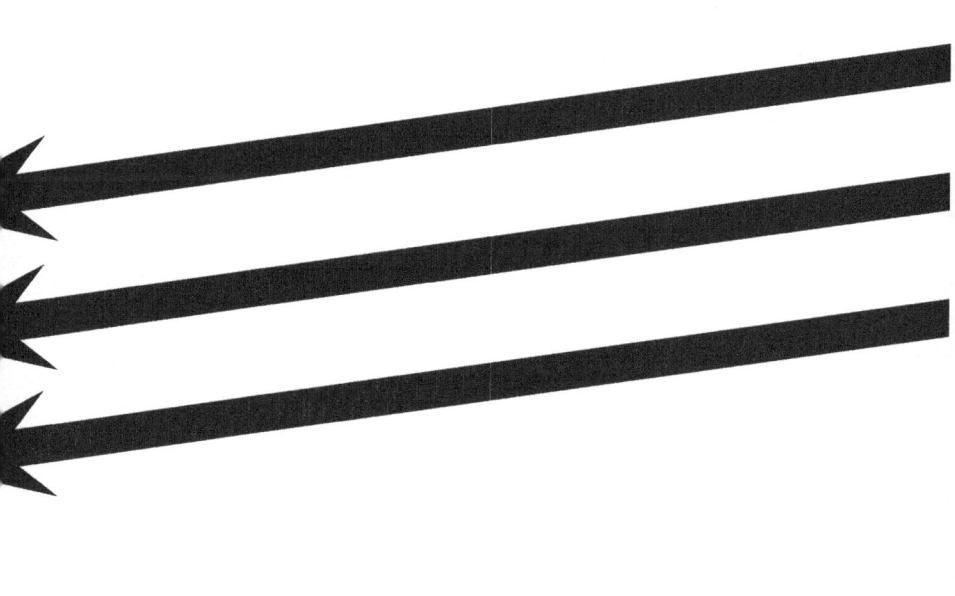

CIVIL INSUBORDINATION, OR WHERE IN AMERIKKKA ARE BLACK PEOPLE SAFE FROM RACISM?

by

henry 7. reneau, jr.

Fish-eyed in the cut, or drunk on Praise Jesus!! Praying their
thousand, thousand mighty prayers, like pouring the river's promise

into stone jars. The crawl space of post-Jim Crow, neither freedom
nor equality, but the lie withholding the Dash-Cam footage,

shows a Chicago cop shooting a black teen 16 times. The automatic
reflex/: if someone is media-labeled *thug/demon /criminal*,

then that is all there is to them. A reflective scatter of storefront glass,
refracting our las' nerve tried—our *less than* plural dichotomy—

looting the liquor store across the street. Always, what feels like salvation,
can be made to sound like savagery. An affinity for disobedience,

like a tangled telephone cord whorl of spiraled down, or

WE ARE ANTIFA

the ballistic ricochet of cause & effect. The riot &

rebellion
a spent shell casing away. All the windows of all the shops,

a drunken glee of mouths with broken teeth. The hidden narrative
like a nicotine fingerprint/: smudged the oily residue of fear, &

abuse, running alongside, or just beneath,
strip mall Amerikkka.

A signpost on the highway/: 13 miles
to the audacity of Hope. A road plowed clean &

gleaming black magnetic,
the gravity of promise. I treated it as a warning

when I entered Integration. The population, *20 & odd Negroes*,
had been crossed out. The pentimento of frayed rope

that dangled an historic threat
from the ancient oak in the town square. Something ominous,

meant to harbinger,
like tadpoles propagating in stagnant water. Between Hallelujah!! &

are we there yet? The pale promise of Hope, before the fire next time.

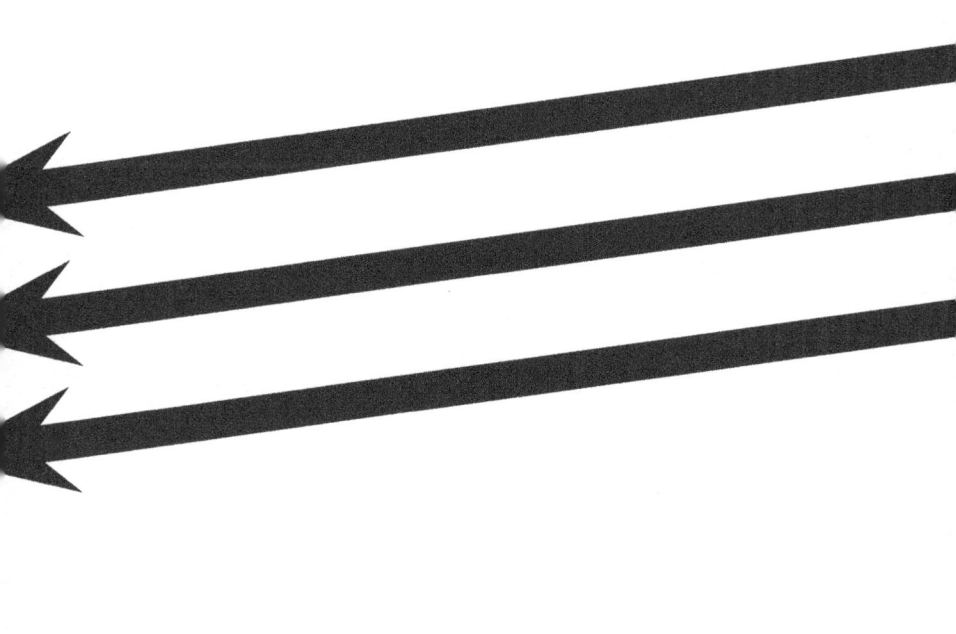

THOUSANDS OF WHITE ALLIES

by

John Streamas

It was a white professor who introduced
me to the term "microaggression," a white
graduate student who defined "racial frames."
Campus swarms with whites who donate to Black Lives
Matter and Asian-Latinx alliances,
who denounce cops killing young black men, protest
pipelines defiling sacred Native lands, and
rally against fascists. They chant "no justice,
no peace" with us, they forward antifa rants
to Facebook, they post flyers showing love to
immigrants and Muslims. They hate what we hate,
love what we love. They are us. Except they are
not us. They mime us. They wear our clothes, listen
to our music, move into our neighborhoods,
our homes, our minds. They colonize us. They are
not like good bacteria. They are not like

friendly ghosts. They are not devil's advocates.
They are the cyanide pills we are taught to
swallow when hope runs out. They are the mission
statement of equivocation. While we are
the very dark at the end of their tunnel.

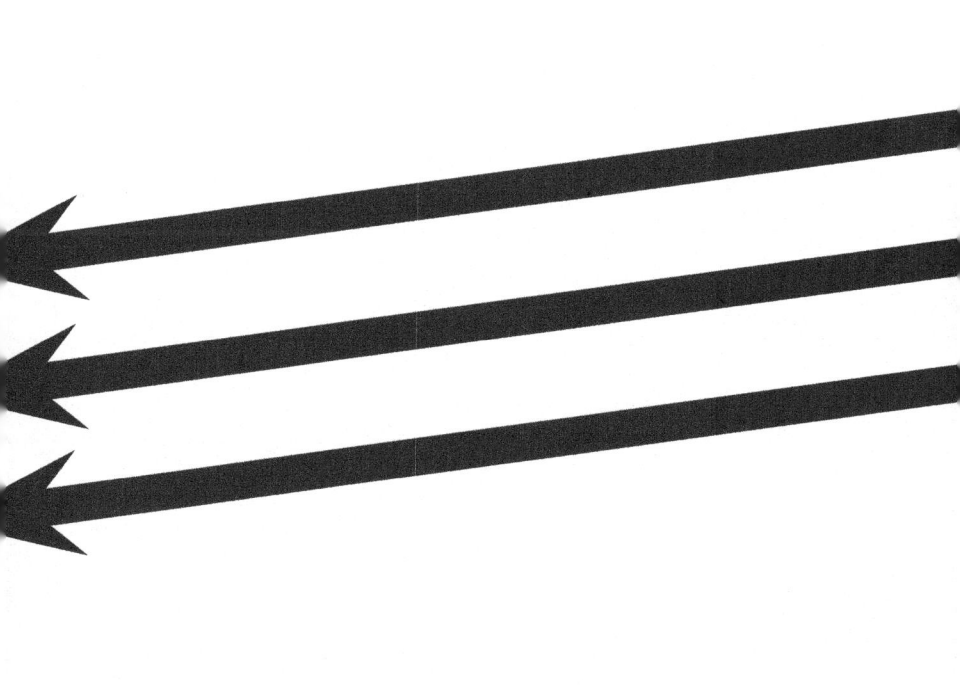

MESSENGERS

by

Richard Hoffman

The house itself, if it had a voice
Would speak out clearly. As for me,
I speak to those who understand;
if they fail, memories are nothing.
  —Aeschylus, *Agamemnon*

We say what we know because we must.
You can cheer us or run us out of town.
It's nothing at first, like rain on dust,

a hairline crack in the faultline's crust,
a tentative first-person plural pronoun.
We say what we know because we must

recall, recount, redeem, and readjust
all that we've known, not for renown.

WE ARE ANTIFA

It's nothing at first, like rain on dust,

or the first few tiny flecks of rust
on barrels buried underground.
We say what we know because we must

talk back to histories we do not trust,
relearn our own, and set them down.
It's nothing at first, like rain on dust.

What does it mean to fear what's just?
You can cheer us or run us out of town.
We say what we know because we must.
It's nothing at first, like rain on dust.

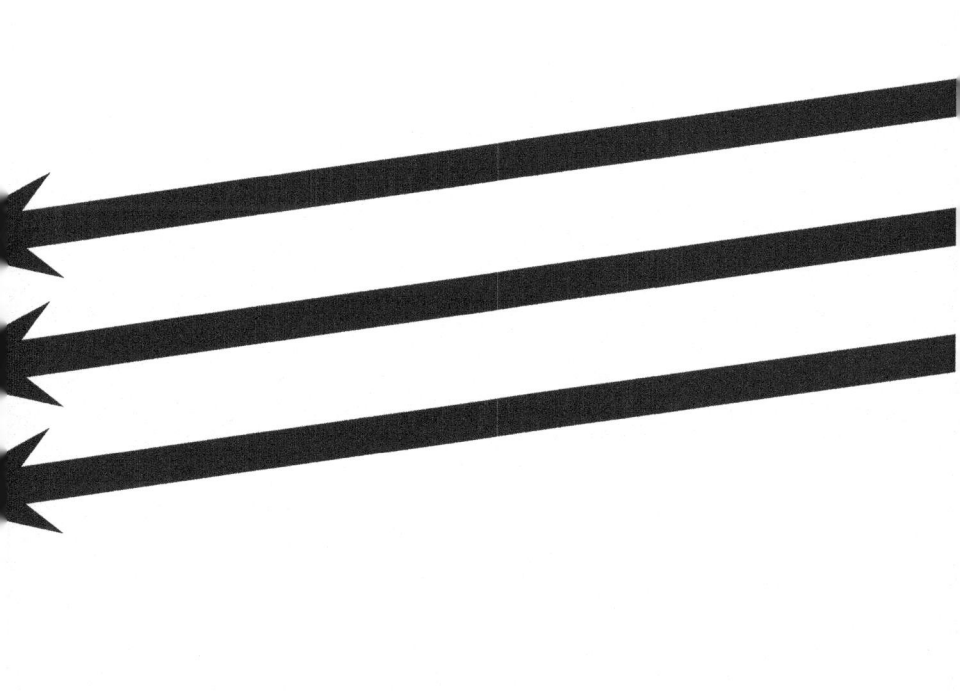

WHITE PRIVILEGE

by

AE Hines

I have been gravely disappointed with the white moderate.
—Rev. Dr. Martin Luther King, Jr., 04/16/1963

If I could, I'd bottle it — open
whatever organ or vein, start filling vials.
Form an assembly line, ship it coast
to coast to every urban center,
every corner convenience store
and give it away for free.

This is not complicated. The man
is dead. The man should not be
dead.

Which is another way of saying:
something is very wrong

with our country.

I will never be a black mother,
never know what it means to lay
a black son to rest, or push a new body
through my own body and weep
at what awaits him.

Is now the time to tell you
I'm white? Is now a good time to say
I have my own brown son?

And what do I tell him? My boy?
Don't run, Son, you might die — but —
don't stop either. Don't run —
they may kill you — or, you run,
my dear sweet boy, you run
like hell. They might kill you
anyway.

I've given up on the world being fair.
Can I instead give my son a card
he can hand the police — a card that says:
My Father Is So White He Glows?
Can I give one to every brown
and black boy in America?
Tell me, and I will charter a plane
and litter them like snow from the skies.

The mayor says, "Please, let there be peace."

WHITE PRIVILEGE

But look at that video — look at all three.
Look at that man again, tell me how
it makes your own heart ache.

I can't even say the man's name. Even that
would be appropriation. I have not earned
the right to that name sitting inside
my embarrassed white mouth.

Which is another way of saying: something
is very, very wrong with our country.

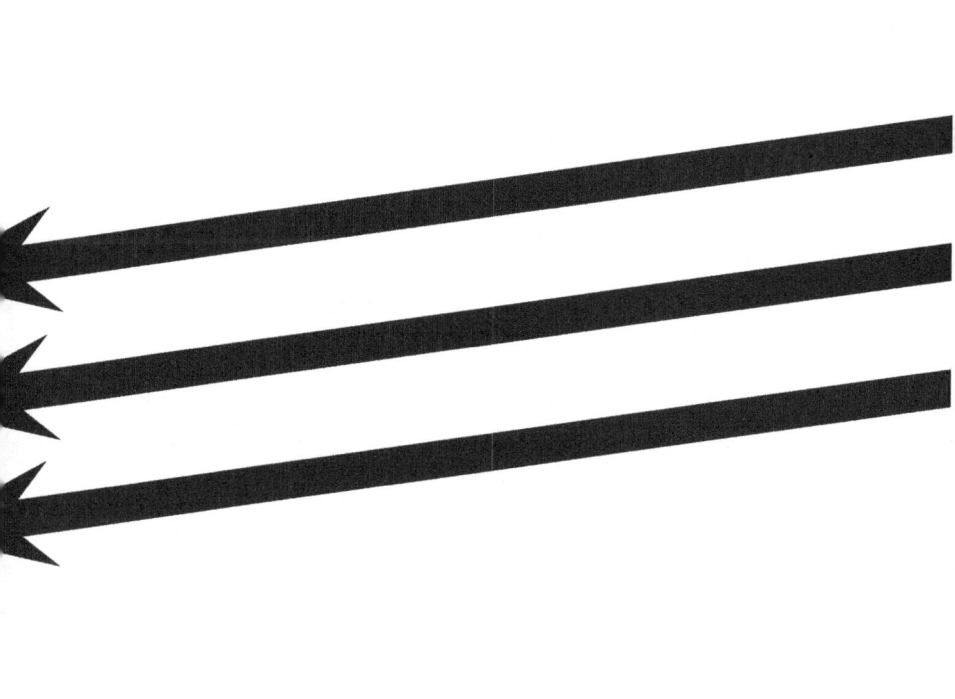

#STEPHONCLARK

by

Nancy Christopherson

Gun gun gun!

A cell phone.
A cell phone.

#STOP. #SHOOTING. #PEOPLE.
Basic hunting rule: ID your target, first.
A cell phone! WTF . . . !
Verify.

#UseHandCuffsNotBullets.
#Less Violence Please.
A broken car window does not prescribe murder.

Not **#SixBulletsInTheBack**.
Not **#Racism**.

Not **#ExcessivePoliceForce**.

#NOMOREGUNS!*$!#&(*!###.

NOT ALL WOLVES

by

Lisa Olsen

You cry "not all cops,"
a protest on behalf of the boys in blue
not yet stained red. After all,
your father was a good man,

your cousin, the embodiment
of protect and serve, and your neighbour,
well, who could blame him?
The kid was reaching into his pocket

and a phone
can look just like a gun. So you bristle
at the generalization, say persecutor
is made persecuted

and it isn't fair. Say it is just

the same as colour sorting
people like crayons,
ignore how some sit pretty

in their box
while others are ground down
and snapped
between ungentle hands.

Not all cops —
but you can't give a child a crayon
and expect him not to use it
wherever he pleases.

You can't walk
into a den of wolves
on faith that maybe some wolves
won't kill to defend their pack.

How good
can an apple be
when the tree is rotten
from the roots?

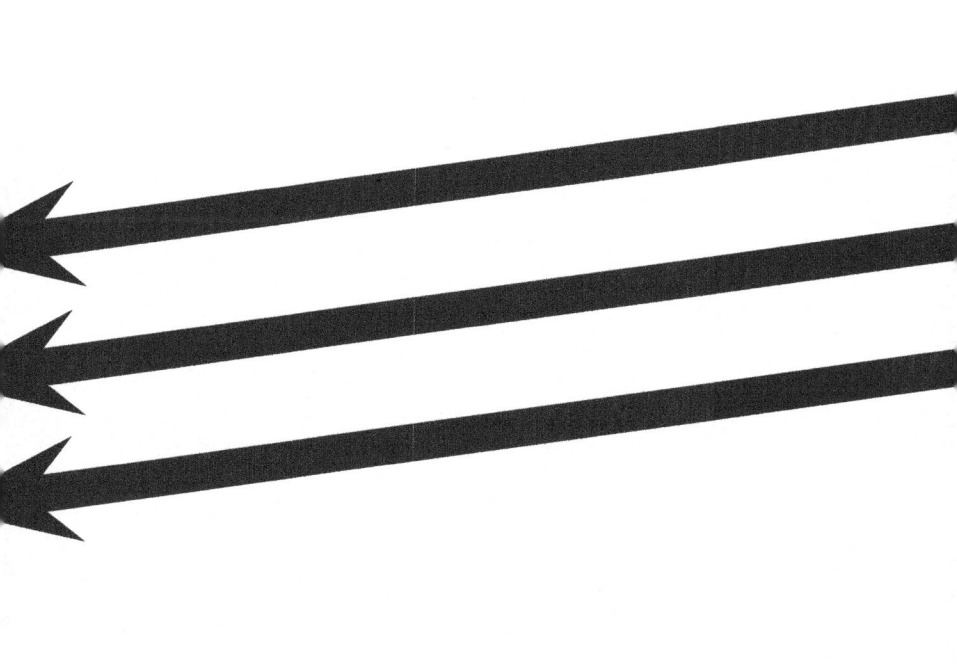

BRUNA BOSCANA, *PARARGE AEGERIA* (LINNAEUS, 1758)

by
Laurence O'Dwyer

Walking over the hills, a stranger asked if I needed a lift.
A shame to turn him down – but I was travelling slowly
from Alaro to Bunyola where Maria Suau Font
was keeping an eye on things, like independence
on the mainland. When I got there, I found a village
in rigor mortis. Sunspots and Aleppo pines;
a church hewn from blocks of sunlight
with a darkroom and a Jesus bug inside.
Bruna Boscana has red and yellow wings;
eyes as black as olives. Maria Suau Font
was an indeterminate age. Her house was full
of Creole music. There was a parabolic mirror
in the front yard: giant petals interleaved like crystal
wings. It was her solar cooker, though it's glassy light
made me think of a Campbell-Stokes recorder,

whose job it is to burn a line on paper,
to record the hours of sunlight.
But there was no need for a weather station in Bunyola –
all you had to do was open your eyes. Sorb apples
and blood-red vines, pomegranates and fruits of thirst;
potatoes like crumbling asteroids. Everything grew
on that island. I settled in, got to know the place.
I woke, I ran, I climbed. Days of gravity and sunstones followed.
From Cala Tuent, the rivers were as dry as rattlesnakes.
It took me a finger of sun to get back to the square.
Dark then, when I heard my name called out.
It was Maria's friends. She was still at work.
They pulled up a chair. A joint was passed around.
The dictionary someone called it – I smoked,
I coughed, I laughed. Linnaeus knew that conspecifics
fight for control of sunspots. But if another species
flies through that light there is no conflict.
I was so tired when I lay down my head that night,
I could see red behind my eyes. It's rare but sometimes
it happens. It's the thrum of veins in the retina.
It's the ripple of a drum; it's the outer limit of sonar.
Rare but precious. Beyond that retina – I know where I am.
It's my Turing test. If it's independence you're after you'll find it
in the sunspots and Aleppo pines where every butterfly
is an anarchist, and every drop of sweat is as wild as honey.

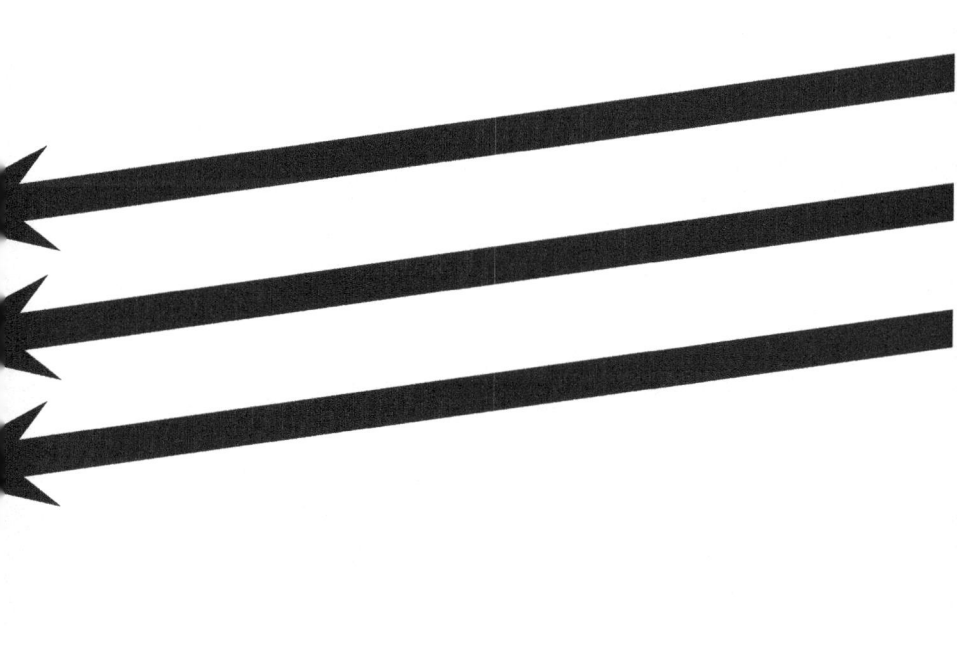

AN OPEN LETTER TO THE SCHOOL RESOURCE OFFICER WHO ALMOST SHOT ME IN MY CLASS

by

Matthew E. Henry

was it the loud noises which drew your attention,
commotion you couldn't process fourteen months
from Afghanistan? a threat too quickly assessed
through the two by three window of my classroom door?
was it my brown arms gesturing wildly, or my beard—
long and unkempt—which obscured thick lips
releasing a language you couldn't easily decipher
(*aggarwayter. pillory. Defarge.*)? was that what triggered
rules of engagement normally absent halls so affluent?
did i seem out of place? did you not notice my shirt and tie?
the matching slacks, socks, and shoes? could you not see
the books open beneath mostly white faces? the smiles
which faltered with your entrance? many missed
your sidearm's slide back to safety as you stumbled
to silence when asked if i could help you. the two
who share my skin saw everything. made eye contact.

held it for two solid seconds. the next day they took to calling me "almost Tamir," while your near-miss story was met with laughter in your squad room.

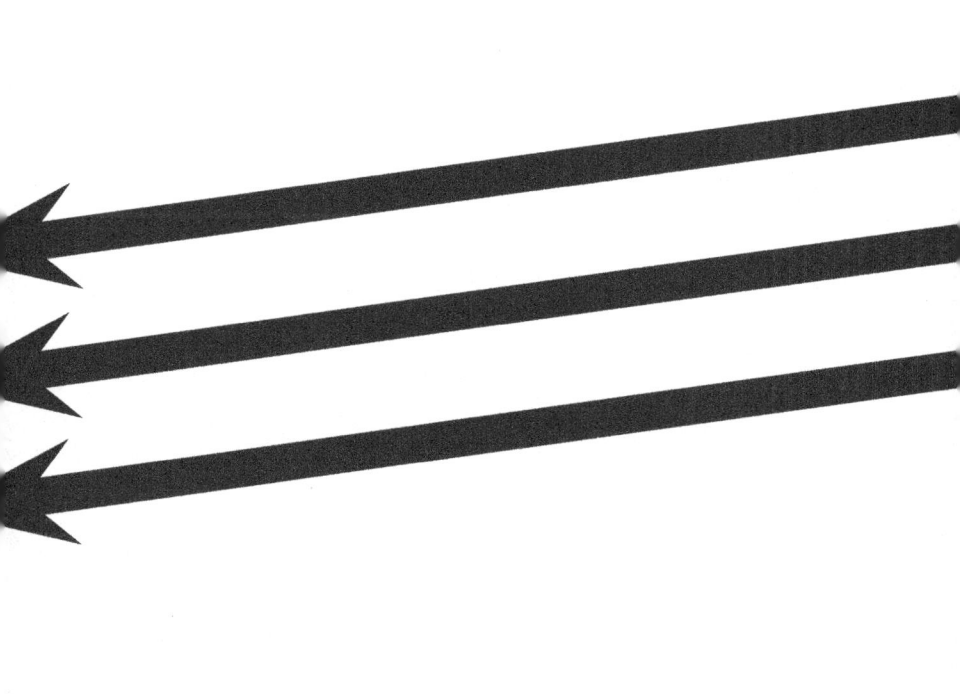

AUTOIMMUNE

by

Vasiliki Albedo

The tree is heavy in
my window. This morning
i see a fist in the branches
i see knees squelching the life out of flowers.
And what do you see,
o body, with your
autoimmune flow that strangles
your radiant organs?
In a consultation a doctor once
called it an exaggerated response.
I'd call it rage, except
it isn't blind when a branch milks
the air out of the darker flowers,
when the fathering limb becomes
a pulmonary fistula that leaves you pleading.
Body remember

you are one,
stop arguing with yourself
take a deep breath, count
to a thousand. All your lives matter
just the same. Your biases
are ulcering the lining
and you wolf yourself down in response,
keep making those paranoid,
blue autoantibodies.
O chronic body, how you mirror
the world. Your joints hurt
systemically at every juncture
and your heart's inflamed with tenderness
a friendly fire that turned sour.
Your mangled parts cog in a perfect glitch
that ticks the same red minute and again
the minute in which you are
both the steel and the rust
the tree and the blight
the new leaf and the dieback.

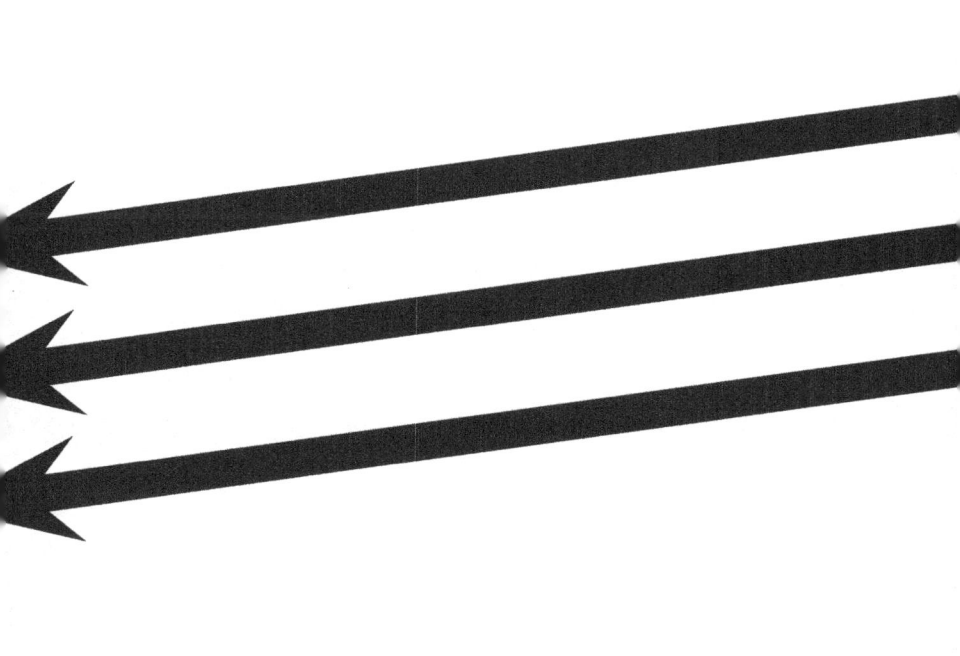

ON SECTARIANISM

by

Mariana Mcdonald

In Argentina death squads killed
ultra, former, and suspected leftists.
Machine guns riddled Trotskyist brains

and Leninist leaders were hunted.
Coke-bottle bodies of militiamen raped
and battered the bodies of nonaligned women.

In North America young Black men
are shot in the streets quite ignorant of Mao,
as non-discriminating wiretaps pry

into the thoughts of thousands.

I would be the first to say
use science and experience together;

study, think, and criticize.

Stand firm on your principles.
But let me, friend, remind you when
you leap to strike that person's thought:

Nonsectarian pools of blood
stain the earth to teach us all
a lesson we're compelled to learn:

the enemy knows who the enemy is.

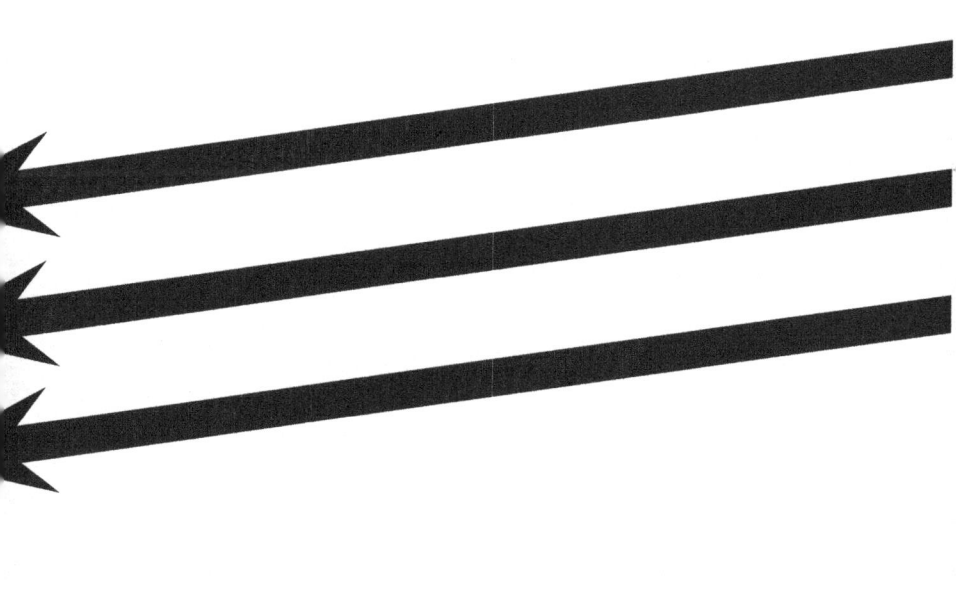

GHETTO YOUTH

by

Darriel McBride

They tell us to hold on.
Keep praying
and change will come.
But ghetto youth don't pray.
We fight.

Violence is a language of its own.
The ghetto is its own world
stitched into a grimy tapestry.
A playground and battlefield
dressed in needles, blunts,
pissy elevators,
broken dreams,
and dead bodies.

Our bodies

WE ARE ANTIFA

still currency.
Our bodies
still in bondage—
cages,
coffins,
pavements
backyards,
classrooms,
subway platforms,
and outside of bodegas.

We are not as promising
as the stock market,
but still overstocked like cattle
in prison cells.
The American Dream?
Or The American Nightmare?

My eyes were made in the Bronx,
but they don't limit my perception.

I'm the rose that grew from the concrete.
I'm from ground zero
where black and brown bodies
still get auctioned like fine jewelry.

Ghetto youth will break your heart
and your face.
Unapologetic with every poisonous word
we spit.

GHETTO YOUTH

Swag on "a hunnit."
These streets
be our
runway and prison yard.

I'm from summers
cooled off by the fire hydrant.
And winters spent
getting dressed for school
in front of the oven.
I'm from broken down kitchens
with leaking roofs.
I'm from welfare lines
and sidewalk
memorials
in a hood near you.

This is that Bronx state of mind.
That New York nationality.
The miseducation of a dope baby.
Daughter of a junkie,
but the perfect matrimony of woke and classy.
So that makes me dope
in every sense of the word.
Ghetto girl.

I'm from a caged neighborhood
ushered by government policies.
I've been casted into a community
that knows pain, anger, and loss

WE ARE ANTIFA

like children should know laughter.

Struggling to survive
the killing fields we call "The Trenches,"
but who built these streets?
Who cooked the crack cocaine?
Who sold and brought in
the pellets of death
that find their way into the bodies
of innocent young dreamers
when we don't have passports?
When the idea of leaving the hood
is a foreign language.

If I showed you a portrait of my life,
what would you make of it?
Would you deem it as equally beautiful
as the abstract lines of blues and reds
that sell for half a million dollars
at the Museum of Modern Art?

Some of us make it out of here,
but the game is always played with faded dice.
So forgetting is what we do best.
And even in our victories
we are still made to feel smaller than the rest.

Every kid
from the ghetto
has a little bit of gangsta in them.

GHETTO YOUTH

But even being tough
is not enough
for a one way ticket
out of the struggle.
No matter where I go
home is still the concrete jungle.

My eyes were made in the hood,
but they don't limit my perception.
The ghetto is its own colorful world
stitched into a *recycled* tapestry.
Now, that's art.
How we always manage to make something
out of nothing.

They tell us to hold on.
Keep praying
and change will come.
But ghetto youth don't pray.
We fight.
They tell us
we should smile more,
but roses don't smile
they die.

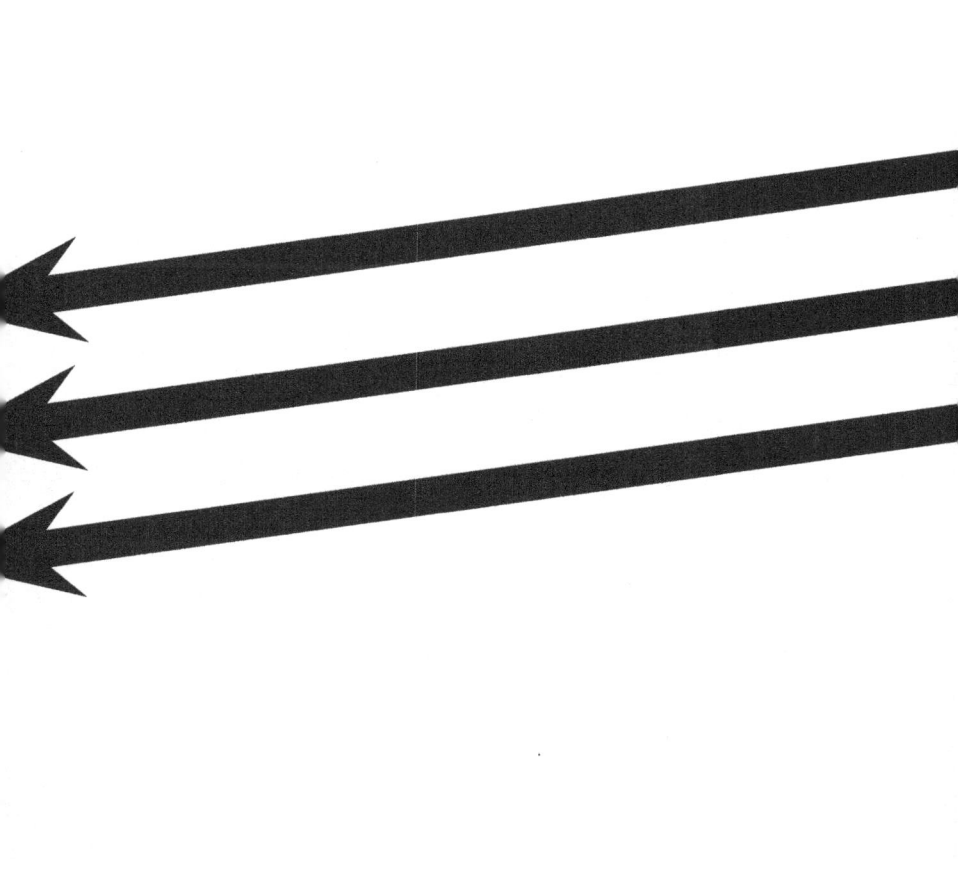

KNEE ON THE NECK

by

Pèlúmi Sàlàkọ́

This uprising will bring out the beast in us.
—Fela Kuti

In the story that invents this poem
a knee takes a dive into my brother's neck

so long he cries out:
I can't breathe, Mama.

Then he died. Four hundred years
you stomp on our faces, Amrikka.

All these years I cry my sadness
to the night, the earth absorbing my tears

without record. Illegal as I am

WE ARE ANTIFA

in this country, I tend your roots,

I sing the anthem with my body still
yet each time you remind me

that I am not human enough.
This violence wreaks my body &

today the stars burst out
to reclaim their place in the sky.

Fire, like bullet, does not wait for consent
before it eats the things in its way.

Today, the night returns to its place
of roost. We link arms and sing

like birds taming the wind,
ascending into the skies.

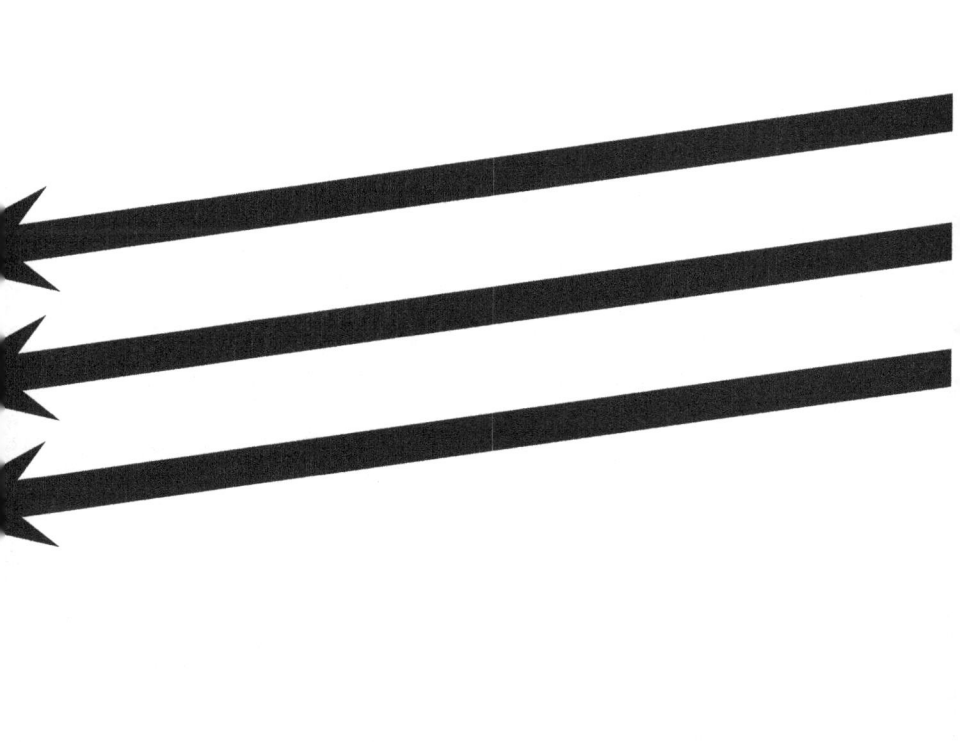

CONTRIBUTORS

Geoffrey Aitken is an emerging poet in South Australia gaining momentum with publishers: *Underground Writers*: Issues 27 & 28 (AUS.), *Glass Journal: Poets Resist* (U.S.), *Flashes of Brilliance* (U.S.), *Aesthetica* (U.K.), *Militant Thistles* (U.K.), *Sparks of Calliope* (U.S.).

Vasiliki Albedo lives in Greece. Her poems have appeared in *Beloit Poetry Journal*, *Ambit*, *The Rialto,* and elsewhere. She has been nominated for Pushcart prizes and was commended in the 2018 National Poetry competition.

Blake L. Bell is finishing up her M.F.A. at Mississippi University for Women and teaching writing at a magnet high school in South Louisiana. She can mostly be found outside on her back patio reading, writing and working in her garden. To read more from her, visit blakelbell.com or follow her @blakelbell.

Gary Bloom grew up in Minneapolis and attended what is now Minnesota State University, Mankato. Articles, photography, and poetry have been published in *Grit, Cappers, Milwaukee Magazine, Colllier's, The Buffalo News, The Grand Rapids Press,*

Oasis, Mankato Poetry Review, and *Black Diaspora.*

Emily Capers lives in Chicago, recently earning a M.F.A. in Fiction there. Capers' writing explores the varieties of self-identity, and has appeared in *Allegory Ridge, High Shelf Press,* and *The Mill.*

Andrés Castro is a P.E.N. member, listed in the *Poet's & Writer's* directory. He keeps a personal blog, *The Practicing Poet: Dialogue to Creativity, Poetry, and Liberation.* He identifies as a Nuyorican with European, Middle Eastern, African, and Indigenous Taino ancestry, and was raised in the South Bronx.

Nancy Christopherson's poems have appeared in *Helen Literary Magazine, Peregrine Journal, Raven Chronicles, Third Wednesday, Verseweavers* and *Xanadu,* among others. Author of *The Leaf,* she lives and writes in eastern Oregon, U.S. Visit nancychristophersonpoetry.com.

Rhea Dhanbhoora worked for a decade as editor and writer in print and digital content for a variety of clients, before moving to New York to get her master's degree, and finally write stories everyone told her no one would read. She's currently working on a collection about women based in the underrepresented Parsi Zoroastrian diaspora.

Connor Drexler lives in Madison, WI. He has pursued many passions in his lifetime, and will always remain a writer.

CONTRIBUTOR BIOS

Charles Duffie is a writer in Los Angeles. His work has appeared in *The Los Angeles Review of Books, So It Goes, Atticus Review, Prime Number Magazine, Role Reboot, Exposition Review,* and others. His stories have been nominated for Pushcart Prizes and Best of the Net Awards.

Jonathan Endurance is a Nigerian poet whose poetry appears in *Rattle, Up the Staircase Quarterly, Alegrarse, FIVE:2:ONE, The Cardiff Review, The Ellis Review, Brittle Paper* and elsewhere.

Jeff Ewing is the author of the short story collection *The Middle Ground*, published by *Into the Void*. His fiction, poetry, and essays have appeared in *Crazyhorse, Southwest Review, ZYZZYVA, Willow Springs, Subtropics, Utne Reader,* and *Saint Ann's Review*. He lives in Sacramento, California.

Joshua Fernandez is a Mexican antifascist living in N. California, who teaches writing, writes satire at *The Hard Times,* and helps run the Sacramento Community Self-Defense Collective.

Rebecca Frost is the southern sister of a multiracial family, the progeny of colonizers and the colonized, and a wannabe detective who's very into unpacking the unyielding hypocrisy littered throughout Southern history. She explores that swamp of contradictions in her research and writing.

Renoir Gaither writes from Saint Paul, MN. A Black poet, anti-capitalist, and abolitionist, he believes only radical imagination and struggle can bring about social justice, not reform. His work has recently appeared in *Crab Fat, Soliloquies anthology, Berkeley Poetry Review,* and *Obsidian: Literature in the African Diaspora.*

Priyanthini Guns was brought up in Scarborough, Tkaronto, Ontario. She manages an arts education organisation which operates in Sri Lanka. She is a writer, sometimes-actress, and a teacher. She's been published in *gal-dem* and anonymously in *The Guardian*'s *Secret Teacher* column. priyaguns.com; @bigcatsguns.

Matt Harris is a writer from Liverpool, U.K., with poetry and short fiction in *HOAX, Confingo, The Alarmist, The Nottingham Review,* and others. horridwithcogs.wordpress.com.

Matthew E. Henry is author of *Teaching While Black* (Main Street Rag, 2020). His recent works are appearing or forthcoming in *Bryant Literary Review, New Verse News, Ninth Letter, Ploughshares, Poemeleon, Rejection Lit, The Revolution (Relaunch), Solstice,* and *Versification.* MEHPoeting.com.

AE Hines is a gay poet originally from rural North Carolina, now residing in Portland, Oregon. He is a recent Pushcart nominee and his work has appeared in numerous publications, including *Atlanta Review, California Quarterly, The Briar Cliff Review, Hawaii Pacific Review, I-70 Review, The Crosswinds Poetry Journal, SLAB,* and *Pinyon.* www.aehines.net.

Richard Hoffman has published four volumes of poetry, most recently *Noon until Night,* which won the 2018 Massachusetts

CONTRIBUTOR BIOS

Book Award. His other books include the memoirs *Half the House* and *Love & Fury*, and the story collection *Interference and Other Stories*. He is Senior Writer in Residence at Emerson College, and nonfiction editor at *Solstice: A Magazine of Diverse Voices*.

Daniel Nathan Horn has been a farmhand, a U.S. Marine, an engineer. His writing has been shortlisted for the Into the Void Fiction Prize. He currently resides in San Diego and attends the Drexel University M.F.A. in Creative Writing low residency program.

Ramon Jimenez is an educator and writer from Seattle, Washington. Originally from Los Angeles, Ramon works as a high school social studies and language arts teacher. Ramon's poems are featured in *Rigorous Magazine* and *The Anti-Languorous Project*.

Tim Jones is a fiction writer living in N. California. He grew up in the Detroit area, and though he does not remember the 1967 riot there, it informed and shaped the world he came to know.

Edward Moreta Jr. (he/him/his) is an Afro-Latino student in the college class of 2022. He is from Dorchester in the Greater Boston Area and has been published in *The Offing* and *Tahoma Literary Review*.

henry 7. reneau, jr. writes words of conflagration to awaken the world ablaze, an inferno of free verse illuminated by his affinity for disobedience, like a discharged bullet that commits a felony every day, the spontaneous combustion that blazes from his heart, phoenix-fluxed red & gold, exploding through change is gonna come to implement the fire next time.

A native of The District of Colombia, Lin Lucas' comics and illustrations have appeared in Seattle's weekly paper *The Stranger*, *Top Shelf Comics*, the Xeric Award winning *Two-Fisted Science*, *The Psychology of Race*, French anthology *Le Dernier Neurone*, and *Split Rock Review*. Lin lives and teaches in Tucson, Arizona.

Thea Matthews is a poet, and author of *Unearth [The Flowers]*. She is Afrolatinx with Black, Indigenous, and Mexican blood who writes on the complexities of humanity, grief, and resiliency. Her work has appeared in *Atlanta Review, The Rumpus, Foglifter*. She is a first-year M.F.A. candidate at New York University.

Darriel McBride is a poet and activist from the South Bronx, New York. She graduated from Marist College in 2017 with a Bachelors in English Writing. She is a U.S Fulbright Alumni and Gates Millennium Scholar. Darriel's poetry has been featured in *Bronx Native Writer's Anthology* Vol. 1 and *LUNA*.

Mariana Mcdonald is a poet, writer and scientist. She co-authored with Margaret Randall the recently released *Dominga Rescues the Flag*, the story of Black Puerto Rican heroine Dominga de la Cruz. Mcdonald is active in social justice movements and the writing community.

Alan Meyrowitz retired in 2005 after a career in computer research. His writing has appeared in *Dark Ink* anthology, *Eclectica*,

CONTRIBUTOR BIOS

Esthetic Apostle, Existere, From Whispers to Roars, Inwood Indiana, Jitter, The Literary Hatchet, The Nassau Review, Poetry Quarterly, Schuylkill Valley Journal, Shark Reef, Shroud, Spirit's Tincture.

Michael J Moore's books include *Highway Twenty*, which appeared on the Preliminary Ballot for the Bram Stoker Award, and the bestselling post-apocalyptic novel, *After the Change*, which is used as curriculum at the University of Washington. His work has received awards and appeared in various anthologies, journals, newspapers (including *Huffington Post*), and has been adapted for theatre.

Laurence O'Dwyer holds a Ph.D. in Paradigms of Memory formation from Trinity College, Dublin. His first collection of poetry, *Tractography* (Templar, 2018) received the Straid Collection Award. In 2019 he received the Van Cleef & Arpels Special Fellowship in Poetry from the Bogliasco Foundation. He has received fellowships from The MacDowell Colony and the Rensing Center, in addition to the Yeovil Prize for Poetry and the Patrick Kavanagh Award for Poetry.

Kanyinsola Olorunnisola is an experimental poet, essayist and writer of fiction. His work has appeared in *Popula, Barren, Bodega, Gertrude, Headline, Brittle Paper, Arts and Africa, The Account, On the Seawall, Bakwa, Bombay Review*. He won the 2016 Albert Jungers Poetry Prize and the 2017 Fisayo Soyombo Essay Prize.

Lisa Olsen lives in Ottawa with her partner and their two cats.

She teaches English as a second language. She is Antifa.

Sam Palmer is a Humanities secondary school teacher from Staffordshire, U.K. She is a short story and flash fiction writer. She particularly likes to write about relationships and families, often with women as a focus.

Cree N. Pettaway is a Southern, Black writer from Mobile, Alabama, with stories published in *Parhelion, West Texas Literary Review,* and *Oyster River Pages.* creepettaway.com.

Jonathan Andrew Pérez, Esq. is a senior attorney in social justice, and teaches a course at Wesleyan university titled Poetic Justice: Race, the Law, and Structural Injustice through The Word.

James Redfern was born and raised in Long Beach, California. A graduate of Grinnell College, his work has been published in *The American Journal of Poetry, Transcend, Verity La: The Clozapine Clinic, Dime Show Review, Swimming with Elephants, Montana Mouthful, Anti-Heroin Chic, Great Lakes Poetry Press, Fear and Loathing in Long Beach,* and elsewhere.

M. J. Ridley is an undergraduate student at Allegheny College. She is working towards an English (creative writing emphasis) major, with environmental writing and education minors. She hopes to become an English teacher at the high school level.

Pèlúmi Sàlàkọ́ presently studies for a Bachelor of Arts in

History and International Studies. His writings have appeared or are forthcoming in *Jacarpress, The Rising Phoenix Review, Palette Poetry, Down River Road,* and elsewhere.

Larry Smith is the editor-director of Bottom Dog Press in Ohio, and a poet and fiction writer.

Born in Tokyo to a war bride, John Streamas is an associate professor of ethnic studies and American studies at Washington State University. His poetry and prose are published or forthcoming in *Asian American Literary Review, Spillway,* Akashic Books' *Fri-Sci Fi* webpage, and elsewhere. He is a proud charter member of the fascist Professor Watchlist.

Josh Wagner is a novelist and playwright from Missoula, Montana, with a Creative Writing M.Sc. from the University of Edinburgh. He is the author of four novels and three graphic novels, and has won awards for his work in comics and theatre. His short stories and poetry have been published by *Cafe Irreal, Not One of Us (Clarity), Medulla Review, Lovecraft eZine, Cleaver Magazine, Asymmetrical Press,* and *Image Comics.*

Bill Wilkinson writes fiction from his home in northwestern Pennsylvania.

Made in the USA
Monee, IL
03 May 2026

49438462R00173